Leo Strauss and the Politics of American Empire

Leo Strauss

AND THE

Politics

OF

American

Empire

Anne Norton

YALE UNIVERSITY PRESS   NEW HAVEN & LONDON

Designed by Rebecca Gibb.
Set in Janson text type by Integrated Publishing Solutions.
Printed in the United States of America.

The Library of Congress has cataloged the hardcover edition as follows:
Norton, Anne.
Leo Strauss and the politics of American empire / Anne Norton.
p. cm.
Includes index.
ISBN 0-300-10436-7 (cloth : alk. paper)
1. Strauss, Leo. 2. Conservatism—United States. 3. United States—Intellectual
life—20th century. 4. Political science—Philosophy. 5. Political science—
History. I. Title.
JC251.S8N67 2004
320′.092—dc22
2004010799

A catalogue record for this book is available from the British Library.

The paper in this book meets the guidelines for permanence and durability
of the Committee on Production Guidelines for Book Longevity
of the Council on Library Resources.

ISBN 0-300-10973-3 (pbk. : alk. paper)

10 9 8 7 6 5 4 3 2

Interpretation

Leg' ich mich aus, so leg' ich mich hinein:
Ich Kann nicht selbst mein Interprete sein.
Doch wer nur steigt auf seiner eignen Bahn,
Trägt auch mein Bild zu hellerm Licht hinan.

Friedrich Nietzsche

Interpreting myself, I always read
Myself into my books. I clearly need
Some help. But all who climb on their own way
Carry my image, too, into the breaking day.

(Translated by Walter Kaufmann)

Contents

Preface

I am the student of Joseph Cropsey, who was the student of Leo Strauss, with whom he edited the *History of Political Philosophy*. I am the student of Ralph Lerner, who was the student of Strauss. I studied with Leon Kass and watched Allan Bloom teach. I know many Straussians, and some of the students of Strauss, very well. Because I am bound within those networks, I know others linked to them. I write this book because I have debts to pay and ghosts to lay, and because I was made, somewhat against my will, the carrier of an oral history.

From the time that I first came to the University of Chicago, professors took me aside to tell me stories of Strauss and the Straussians. I did not ask for these stories, and I often wondered why my professors told them to me. If they wanted to tell me stories, I preferred others. Joe Cropsey told me stories about his campaigns in the deserts of North Africa and the invasion of Italy. Leonard Binder told me of the 1948 war and the fighting in Jerusalem. Ari Zolberg had stories of being a Jewish child in Belgium and the Netherlands: of being almost caught, and saved again in the most generous and improbable ways during the war; then after, of such comparatively trivial hardships as eating eggs cooked in peanut butter. Like the military men of my childhood they told these stories very lightly. The war as Cropsey told it had intervened to spare him the fate—more feared if not more fearsome—of writing his dissertation on a subject that had gone cold for him. In Zolberg's account, the chief of police provided false papers, Jesuit priests hid Jewish children, German soldiers warned of Nazi sweeps. Binder laughed about the Arabic he learned as a prisoner. They told me these things, and they talked to me about philosophy and revolution, but more often they told me about Strauss and the Straussians.

Cropsey told me how he had returned from the war to have Strauss teach him, as he said, how to read. Zolberg told me of the Straussian truth squads and the conflicts in the department. Binder told me of Strauss's insistence on being taken to seminars in anthropology, with their slides of scantily clad natives and accounts of exotic sexual practices.

As one professor saw me taken into another's office, he (they were all men then, all but Susanne Rudolph, who never did this sort of thing) would find me and tell me to come and talk to him, or take me in on the spot and tell me his account of what he imagined the other had told me. After a while I realized that the stories I heard without real interest were very much sought after by other students, even by other professors. Though I didn't value the stories, I did take pleasure in being set apart. If I was not curious about Strauss, I began to be curious about his circle: about the desire of my professors and the older students to tell me stories, to make sure that I had their version, to warn me of one another. I was curious about the passion they brought to these stories, and the effort they took to convey both the passion and the stories to me. I saw no reason for it at the time.

In the years afterward I forgot many of the stories. I saw Straussians often enough. They were my professors and fellow students first; later they were colleagues, members of another school of thought in political theory, a school I knew but whose views I did not share. I would never have thought of writing about them, but things changed. Certain of the people I had known came to power. The nation went to war. Because the nation is at war, and because the Straussians are prominent among those who govern, the accounts I had been given are no longer part of a curious personal history but elements of a common legacy. In remembering that past, I came to see the shapes of two futures.

Acknowledgments

This is a book I chose to write, but I was asked to write it. The idea for the book, and many suggestions along the way, came from John Kulka, my editor at Yale University Press. John conceived the book, persuaded me to do it, shaped and shepherded it. I'm grateful to him for our conversations, for his help, and for his commitment. I am also grateful for the detailed and perceptive comments on the proposal from an anonymous reader for the Press, and to Dan Heaton for his editing. Many people helped me in writing this book. Some I can thank; in other cases, I think my thanks would be a burden and so a poor return for all their help. I may not place people in the right camp, and I apologize. Jeff Tulis told me to study with Cropsey when I first went to Chicago. Deborah Harrold took many of the same classes and remembered the people and the stories. Rogers Smith, Victoria

Hattam, Ellen Kennedy, Mary Ann Gallagher, and George Shulman read the manuscript on very short notice and generously provided crucial and invaluable advice. I am indebted to them for their friendship above all, and for many other things, but no one should make the mistake of thinking that they agree with all that I have written. Eric Feigenbaum was a superb research assistant. The Franke Center for the Humanities at the University of Chicago provided me with the opportunity to present an abridged version of the book to an informed, critically acute, and welcoming audience. The Alfred L. Cass Term Chair provided funds for research. I regret any trouble that comes to anyone for their involvement with me, and that I cannot fully acknowledge all the people on whom I relied.

Leo Strauss and the Politics of American Empire

Prelude

From outside the circle of the Straussians, their influence appears like a triumphant freemasonry, a kabbalistic circle, a troop of intellectual Templars directing (largely from behind the scenes) an unsophisticated and parochial Court. From within, the influence of the Straussians reads differently: as the ascendance of virtue, the reward of patience, the presence of a generous philosophy in politics, the triumph of the tough-minded.

Outside the academy, the questions raised in political theory seem to have been cultivated in an academic hothouse: fragile, ornamental, and unproductive, unsuited to the rough climate of the world outside. From within they seem like grenades, smooth and hard, ready to launch death and destruction, ready to tear the world apart.

Three stories are interwoven here. There is the story of Leo

Strauss, a philosopher of the University in Exile, who taught American students a new way (that was a very old way) to read a text, who carried European philosophy into a new world. Then there is the story of the Straussians, which is properly two stories: the story of the philosophic lineage that came from Leo Strauss, and the story of a set of students taking that name, regarded by others—and regarding themselves—as a chosen set of initiates into a hidden teaching. These latter, and lesser, Straussians were bound not simply by descent from a common teacher or a love of learning. They were bound by politics as well: a distinctly and distinctively conservative politics. They came to power and have influenced the character of governance in the United States. This is also, therefore, a story of American conservatism.

The final story, and the most important, is the story of America in question: a nation made a moral battleground. Here we find some of the questions Strauss posed, asked in another way. Is America to be guided by reason or the revealed word of God? Has the reach of the mind in science, the reach of the hand in technology, gone beyond limits set by nature? With all the tools and the pleasures of modernity at hand, are we too complaisant and too comfortable?

As I write this, America is at war. Our troops occupy Iraq and serve in Afghanistan. In Iraq they are frequently attacked. In Afghanistan, the government and the peace are insecure. These, we are told, are merely battlefields in a greater war: the war against terror. War was once a matter of simple questions: Who are our friends? Who is the enemy? In this war the enemy is un-known, uncertain. Not knowing the enemy, we cannot know when or how or whether victory will come. We cannot know where or when or whether the enemy will strike, or how the na-tion is to be defended. We do not know the enemy. We have found that we do not know ourselves. We were once a republic. Have we become an empire? What is our work in the world? The ancient imperative "Know thyself" carved in Delphi and carried in the heart, came with philosophy from the old world to the new. The questions of that ancient philosophy challenge our present politics.

I *Who Is Leo Strauss? What Is a Straussian?*

Leo Strauss was a political philosopher. He was born a Jew in Germany in 1899 and came to the United States as a refugee in 1938. Strauss found a place in what was called the University in Exile at the New School for Social Research. He later taught, for many years, at the University of Chicago. Before he came to the United States he had written on Spinoza, on Maimonides, and on Carl Schmitt's book *The Concept of the Political*. He later wrote on Xenophon, Plato, al Farabi, Machiavelli, and Aristophanes. He was said to be a timid man, wary of physical harm, who was not very good at managing the practical matters of daily life. On his office wall he had a copy of Dürer's etching of a young rabbit. He told a student that the rabbit, knowing that harm surrounds him, sleeps with his eyes open.

Strauss read and taught as political theorists have done from time immemorial. He would read a passage in a text and ask: "What does it mean?" "Why is this said?" "Why is this said in this way, with these words?" "Why is this said here, in this passage, rather than earlier or later?" He would also ask: "What is not said here?" In the *shul* and the *madrasa*, in seminaries and Bible study groups, sacred texts are still studied in this way. Political theorists read with the same passion and care, and often in the same way. When Strauss came to the United States, this way of reading had fallen out of favor in the universities.

Strauss had many students. Some studied with him formally, others outside the classroom. Those I have met feel deeply indebted to him. They talk with remembered pleasure of the first time they heard him teach. Often they say of him, "He taught me to read." Some of them read texts with the same care and skill and grace they say Strauss brought to them: Joseph Cropsey and Ralph Lerner at the University of Chicago, Harvey Mansfield at Harvard, Stanley Rosen at Boston University, Stephen Salkever at Swarthmore. They have taught many people. Some of those they taught have gone into politics.

Strauss also has disciples. These are the people who call themselves Straussians. There is sometimes an element of discipleship in a student, so there is some overlap between these categories. There is very little overlap between the two conditions. Throughout this book, I will distinguish between the students of Strauss, political theorists interested in Strauss's work (some of whom were and others were not students of Strauss), and these disciples. I am sorry for the name "Straussian" because it implicates Strauss in views that were not always his own, but it is best to call people what they call themselves. Straussian is the name these disciples have taken. The Straussians have made a conscious and deliberate effort to shape politics and learning in the United States and abroad.

There are Straussian genealogies and Straussian geographies. Straussian geography divides the country between East and West Coast Straussians. This places Chicago at the center. One Straussian wrote of his move from New York to Chicago that he had been sent from "the provinces" to "the big leagues." Chicago is also sometimes (and more modestly) placed in the East. The East Coast Straussians are said to be more philosophical and less concerned with politics. The dominant intellectual figures among the East Coast Straussians are Joseph Cropsey of Chicago and Harvey Mansfield of Harvard. Both are respected political philosophers. Both are conservative. Harvey Mansfield taught Francis Fukuyama, author of *The End of History*, and William Kristol, editor of the *Weekly Standard*. Joseph Cropsey taught Paul Wolfowitz and Abram Shulsky, both prominent members of the defense establishment. Mansfield is the more political of the two, considering himself—rightly—a conservative activist. Cropsey rarely mentions politics in class. Mansfield baits and battles leftists and liberals, and writes on manners and manliness. My colleague Rogers Smith tells me that if you wish to study with Mansfield you are expected to be a conservative as well. If you are not, you are sent to study with someone else. He has, however, acted generously to scholars who are not conservative.

The West Coast Straussians are prone to zealous partisanship in politics and the academy. The dominant figure among the West Coast Straussians is Harry Jaffa. Jaffa taught for many years at Claremont Graduate School and remains affiliated with the Claremont Institute for the Study of Statesmanship and Political Philosophy. They are regarded as vehement and ideological, even by fellow conservatives, and they are unabashedly partisan. Jaffa writes: "The salvation of the West must come, if it is to come, from the United States. The salvation of the United States, if it is to come, must come from the Republican Party. The salvation of the Republican Party, if it is to come, must come from the conservative party within it." West Coast Straussians regard themselves as combative—"combative as hell," Thomas West, one of their number, writes. They not only dislike liberals, leftists, and Democrats, they have fights to pick with the followers of other conservative figures: Frederick Hayek, Ayn Rand, and Willmoore Kendall. For these men—they are, as far as I know, all men—politics comes before philosophy.

There is another intellectual school that will be important to this account. One might think of it as a Straussian cadet line. This is the school of thought associated with Albert Wohlstetter. Wohlstetter was a political scientist and a colleague of Strauss's at Chicago. He was a scholar of international relations who developed a particular expertise in nuclear strategy. Like Nathan Leites, a scholar of international relations in the grand tradition and another colleague of Strauss's at Chicago, Wohlstetter worked at the Rand Corporation and served as a government consultant on matters of defense strategy.

During the Vietnam war, I am told, Strauss became closer to Leites and Wohlstetter. They had students in common, most notably Paul Wolfowitz. Contact with Leites and Wohlstetter turned the minds of Straussian scholars to patterns and issues in international relations. They found common ground in questions of sovereignty, power, and the characteristic conditions of modernity.

You can find the East and West Coast Straussians, and other variants and subspecies, on a website the Straussians keep for themselves: Straussian.net. Elaborate, well-maintained, and regularly revised, the site provides lists of teachers "in the Straussian tradition" and accounts of Straussians in the news. There is a biography and a bibliography of Leo Strauss, with a list of references to the secondary literature. There is an audio clip from one of Strauss's lectures. There is a discussion site, and a place to contribute to reviews of Straussian classes and Straussian teachers. There are links to other Straussian sites. Perhaps the most charming aspect of the site is the decision to adorn it with modern paintings of classical scenes: a gesture that captures the forms the ancients take in the modern imagination.

For a newcomer, the site is puzzling in several respects. One of these is political. The site is unabashedly conservative, with links to right-wing sites, favorable reviews of right-wing websites and articles, and some unattributed political graphics of its own. The *New York Times* caricature of Paul Wolfowitz in full classical fig is displayed with the photograph of an elderly Leo Strauss. Yet the uninitiated person who comes to the site with simple curiosity, hoping to learn why conservatives find Leo Strauss especially congenial, or hoping to discover the conservative elements in Strauss's thought, will go away unsatisfied. You can learn that Allan Bloom appeared on *Oprah*, you can read Straussian reviews of Hollywood movies, but you will look in vain for an explanation of the determined conservatism of the Straussians.

Political conservatism is, however, a critical element of the way in which Straussians present themselves. The list of "teachers in the Straussian tradition" contains a number of people who have little or no apparent connection to the work or intellectual lineage of Leo Strauss but who have notably conservative political preferences. Others trained by Strauss or in the Straussian lineage, or who teach in the Straussian style but whose politics are liberal or left rather than conservative, are unmentioned.

There are—as one could learn from Straussian.net—some schools that form the background for the story of the Straussians. These schools have professors who studied with Strauss or his students, and who read texts and teach in the Straussian manner. Often they have a great books program or a "core curriculum" in which students are required to study works in the canon of political philosophy. Chicago, Claremont, and St. John's have the added distinction (shared by the New School, emphatically not a Straussian school) of being places Strauss taught.

Academics think of the University of Chicago, Harvard University, and the University of Toronto simply as places where one might learn political theory. Straussians think of them as Straussian schools. No one would be surprised to learn that many prominent Straussians now in government posts got their degrees at Harvard. Harvard prides itself on what the generous call a tradition of public service. Those less generous would say that Harvard is a way station on the road from privilege to power. Several prominent conservatives (especially in the administration of the younger Bush) got their Ph.D.s at the University of Chicago as well. This is more surprising. The University of Chicago is a place deliberately distant from privilege and power, conscious of itself as committed solely to the life of the mind. At Chicago power is suspect, privilege in bad taste. How Chicago became a center for the export of conservative scholars is, in part, a story of the prejudices of the academy, left and right, American and German.

There are Straussian foundations, or, more precisely, foundations which have a particular regard for Strauss and the students of Strauss: Earhart, Olin, Scaife, and the Lynde and Harry Bradley Foundation. They fund fellowships and internships for graduate students, postdoctoral fellowships, and fellowships for senior scholars. There are book subsidies, honoraria, fellowships designed to give young conservative scholars time to write, fellowships reserved for conservative scholarship and the advancement of conservative ideas, and subsidies offered to presses—and student newspapers—to represent "the conservative point of view." They provide research funds, book subsidies, and money for conferences. Some—perhaps all—of these foundations have given money to nonconservatives. Some have given money to me. They prefer, however—as they make clear in their mission statements, application materials, and programs—to give money to conservatives, and they give generously.

Despite this largess, conservatives complain that the academy is hostile territory: that few academics are conservative and that conservatives are less likely to be hired. I think they are right, though the patterns of discrimination are more complex—and less pervasive—than they suggest. Louis Hartz, the great theorist of American political development, famously argued that America was the nation of Lockean liberals, and that the political spectrum did not extend very far to the right or left. I have never heard a colleague say, "That candidate shouldn't be hired; he is a conservative." There are prominent conservative scholars throughout the academy, though they are (like leftists) far rarer than liberals. I have, however, heard colleagues say, "We can't hire him, he is a Straussian."

This is more surprising than it might sound. The American academy holds strongly to the view that politics ought not to interfere with intellectual judgments, that the academy is richer when contending political views are present. People have their prejudices, of course. If they act on them, they usually do so discreetly. More often they try to overcome them. They rarely own them publicly. To do so, even when the prejudice is shared, is regarded as a lapse of intellectual integrity.

Straussians are excluded, those who do the excluding will tell you, because they are a cult. Those who would reject them argue that Straussians have no respect for other academics, that they refuse to read the work of other scholars. They argue that a Straussian will hire no one but another Straussian. They will tell you that Straussians seek to convert students into disciples. They will tell you that they are not persecuting Straussians, they are preventing Straussians from persecuting others.

The number of Straussians in the academy (see Straussian.net) suggests that this persecution has not been very successful. The sense of persecution is, however, a defining aspect of the Straussians. In late 2003, when I first visited it, Straussian.net introduced itself this way: "Leo Strauss was the twentieth century's greatest teacher of political philosophy, and this site is dedicated to the Straussian tradition. Its specific intention is to serve as a guide to students caught up in this wonderful, overwhelming, and persecuted academic movement." The sense of persecution runs through the narrative of Strauss and the Straussians, providing a thread that links their history, their ways of teaching and writing, and their present politics. Strauss comes to America as a refugee, escaping the persecution of the Jews in Nazi Germany. In America, Strauss comes to the aid of a persecuted field, rescuing political philosophy from the determined attempts of behaviorism to annihilate it. The sense of persecution links contemporary Straussians to this history. Though they have no need to fear the knock at the door, no need to go into exile, they speak of their own vulnerability, their persecution, far more often and with greater vehemence than Strauss ever spoke of his. The sense of persecution identifies them with Strauss's history, and with elements of wider currents in American culture. Through it, Straussians connect directly with the sense of vulnerability and persecution among fundamentalist Christians and post-Holocaust Jews. They express not only identification with Strauss but a sense of their place in history at the opening of the new millennium.

The phenomenon that has brought the Straussians to the attention of many Americans is, however, an account not of their persecution but of their power. As Straussians themselves note proudly, there have been many Straussians in Washington. One list was supplied by Straussians in a note to a 1999 book entitled *Leo Strauss, the Straussians, and the American Regime*. The list is by no means complete, but it gives one a sense of the number and significance of Straussians in Washington. The authors noted that John Agresto served as deputy and later acting chairman of the National Endowment of the Humanities, William Allen as chairman of the U.S. Civil Rights Commission. Joseph Bessette was acting director of the Bureau of Justice Statistics. Mark Blitz was the associate director of the U.S. Information Agency. David Epstein served in the Department of Defense, Charles Fairbanks as assistant deputy secretary of state for human rights. Robert Goldwin served as special assistant to President Gerald Ford. William Kristol was chief of staff for Vice President Dan Quayle in the administration of the first George Bush. Carnes Lord served on the National Security Council and as Quayle's chief foreign policy adviser. Michael Mablin was associate director of the House Republican Conference. John Marini and Ken Masugi each served as special assistant to the chairman of the U.S. Equal Opportunity Commission. Gary McDowell advised Edwin Meese, attorney general in the Reagan administration. James Nichols was a senior official at the National Endowment for the Humanities. Ralph Rossum and Steven Schlesinger each served as director of Bureau of Justice Statistics. Gary Schmitt headed President Reagan's advisory board on foreign intelligence. Peter Schramm was a senior official in the Department of Education. Abram Shulsky served as director of strategic arms control at the Department of Defense and has held a number of intelligence positions since. Nathan Tarcov served on the State Department policy planning staff and as an adviser to Alexander Haig while Haig was secretary of state under President Reagan. Michael Uhlman served as assistant attorney general in the Ford administration and as special assistant to Ronald Reagan. Jeffrey Wallin served as director of general programs at the National

Endowment for the Humanities. Bradford Wilson was administrative assistant to Chief Justice of the Supreme Court Warren Burger.

There are more prominent and more powerful Straussians in Washington, notably Paul Wolfowitz, now deputy secretary of defense, and Leon Kass, chairman of the President's Council on Bioethics. John Walters served as drug czar under the younger George Bush. Francis Fukuyama has served in Defense. Around these cluster other Straussians. Kass's Council on Bioethics has a predominance of Straussians on the roster and buttresses that influence with a cohort of Straussians among the administrative staff. Alan Keyes, a student of Allan Bloom's, once sought the Republican presidential nomination. Many Straussians not mentioned above teach or have taught in the military academies and war colleges.

The Straussians mentioned—and others we will see more of—have often held more than one government position: sometimes at the same time. They are often involved—and often with other Straussians—in common projects, inside the government and out of it. Several—William Kristol, Robert Kagan, Gary Schmitt, and Paul Wolfowitz among them—are involved in the Project for a New American Century. Wolfowitz and Shulsky are in the Pentagon's Office of Special Projects. Many have worked (and will probably work again) for the Rand Corporation.

Straussians are also prominent in other Washington industries: in think tanks, lobbies, and political action committees. They write for and edit journals and newspapers. They have connections to journals and newspapers abroad. They work for foundations. Their presence is felt in all these venues. Like other government officials, they move between the worlds of government, think tanks, and corporations.

This is no scattered and disorderly influence. There is a powerful and long-standing Straussian presence at several sites. The first is military. Straussians shape policy at the Department of Defense. These include both those, like Paul Wolfowitz, who hold high positions in the Defense Department, and those who serve as consultants. Richard Perle's Trireme Partners and the Rand Corporation figure prominently in that regard. Each has been shaped by Straussians. The influence of Straussians is doubled here. They both have influence on those working within these consulting groups and have a say in which people and ideas move from the consulting groups into the government. Through this process, people who were not educated by Straussians become subject to their influence and enjoy their patronage. A more direct influence operates on the many officers who have been taught, either at the military academies or in the war and staff colleges, by Straussian professors.

Because many of the Straussians come from the University of Chicago, they have old school ties to the students of another Chicago professor, Albert Wohlstetter. Some, like Wolfowitz, studied with Strauss, the students of Strauss, Straussians, and Wohlstetter. Others, like Zalmay Khalilzad, studied with Wohlstetter and came late to the Straussians. Straussians are influential in their own right, but they also profit from their connections to other influential Washington networks.

The necessarily intimate links between defense and intelligence enhance the influence of the Straussians, for Straussians have a prominent place in the intelligence community as well. The most prominent of these is Abram Shulsky, who has written on the advantages of Strauss's teaching for intelligence work in an essay entitled "Leo Strauss and the World of Intelligence (By Which We Do Not Mean *Nous*)." The intelligence community has other Straussians in its ranks. Gary Schmitt has occupied several positions in the intelligence community. Carnes Lord now teaches at the Naval War College. Straussians have also advised congressional committees on intelligence. Each of these sources of influence reinforces and extends the others.

American political discourse at home and overseas has been influenced by a succession of Straussians. The speeches of Republican presidents, vice presidents, and secretaries of defense have been written by Straussians. If we consider William Galston, we should perhaps include the Clinton administration as well. Galston was on the periphery of the Straussian political orthodoxy. He moved a short distance to the left, but farther than a good Straussian was permitted to go, a position that granted entry into a Democratic Party that had moved considerably to the right. Political pundits, seizing on a current phrase, might call this the Republican wing of the Democratic Party. As associate director of the U.S. Information Agency, Mark Blitz, another Straussian, was charged with helping to maintain America's image abroad.

The reach of the presidency has grown with the executive branch. Presidential councils and committees enable the president and his staff to reach into the arts and sciences. Appointments to these, and to the governing boards of government agencies and institutes, extend that reach further. The sciences have felt the influence of the Straussians especially strongly, through the President's Council on Bioethics. The council's mission is not to advance but to judge scholarship: to decide what values should govern scientific policy and scientific research.

The Straussians I see in government were, until very recently, in middle-level positions. In recent years they have come more firmly and more visibly to power. They are especially prominent in defense and intelligence. In the wake of 9/11, after the invasions of Afghanistan and Iraq, with our troops still stationed there, we know that the influence of the Straussians matters. We need to ask where that influence leads. Those in positions of power and influence have tended to dismiss, with anger or amusement, the idea that the intellectual commitments of the Straussians matter to American politics. They ask why education in a certain school or a certain style should matter to anyone at all.

Leo Strauss offered an answer to this question when he wrote the epilogue to an examination of an earlier school of political science. "One might say," Strauss wrote, "that precisely because the new political science is an authority operating within a democracy it owes an account of itself to those who are subjected, or are to be subjected, to it."

2   *The Lion and the Ass*

The academy is a curious place. Time moves more slowly and more swiftly there. Time moves more slowly because more time is visible. Professors know figures long dead more intimately than they know their neighbors or their families. They and their students read ruins, hieroglyphics, layered rocks, dark matter, and old books. They read the alien and the enemy. Christian saints illuminate the gospel by the light of the pagan Aristotle. Time is larger for them, and so it sometimes seems to move more slowly. But those who sit in the company of the dead, who read forgotten books, who have seen worlds come and go in their minds' eyes, may see things before they happen. They have seen those once regarded as wild-eyed radicals become the conservative icons of another day. They have seen yesterday's conservatives become the vanguard of a later revolution. They see patterns, and so they can predict, sometimes, where change will come—before it has begun, before those who think they make the changes have conceived them. Time may move more slowly for them, but they can move more swiftly through time: into the past and into the future.

They are said to live in "an ivory tower" removed from the world, and in some respects they do. They often look at one part of the world devotedly, hungrily, and ignore the rest, giving their entire mind to the workings of a single enzyme, or the thinking of Jean-Jacques Rousseau. Because their sense of time is long, they are often indifferent to the things around them. Yet they often know the world very well, far better than those who think professors are confined to an ivory tower. They see their colleagues and those they work for, as other working people do. They see their students, and they see others: those whose lives they know through their scholarship. They often speak other languages. They read and write, study, eat, and make friends, in several places—in Boston and Bangladesh, for example; in Azerbaijan and Athens, Georgia. They may have a home and a life in the United States, and another in the place where they work— whether that is a working-class mill town in eastern Ohio or a palace in Jaipur. They have often come from still another place: from another mill town, an army post in Kansas, or the suburbs of Orange County.

Leo Strauss went from Marburg and Freiburg to London and New York; from Germany to England and America; from the old world to the new. He went from a world dissolving in war to a world newly made as a great power. He went from Freiburg and New York to Athens and Jerusalem, to the Cairo of Saladin and the Philadelphia of the Founders. For us Chicago stands as the center of these journeys. Strauss settled in Chicago, taught, and made himself remembered there. Chicago still stands at the center of the Straussian world.

The first students of Strauss I knew at Chicago were my professors Joseph Cropsey and Ralph Lerner. To listen to them read a text was to go into a garden, into a wilderness, into an ocean and breathe. They were scandalous, they were daring, they took your breath away with their honesty. They were precise, disciplined, ascetic, reverent, heretical, blasphemous, and fearless. Nothing stopped them, nothing at all. Often it went entirely unnoticed. There would be an unfinished quotation or a pun and in it the cleverest, wittiest heresy. There would be a discreet allusion or a simple statement, and one would find oneself at the edge of the abyss. Perhaps this is the origin of the idea of secret teachings. If so, I can tell you, there were no secret teachings; it was all done in the open. I imagine a good deal of it is on tape.

Cropsey taught, in my time, in a bare auditorium in Pick Hall, gray and cold. He was a tall, thin man, who has looked the same from that day to this. He came into the room and began to lecture in a monotone. There were little men in the front who would scurry into action with tape recorders. I was told that they had taped Strauss. Now they were taping Cropsey. They were very old grad students, even for Chicago, very clerkish, very Dickensian, and rather pathetic. Even those of the Straussians who thought their presence conferred a sort of distinction on the proceedings felt a certain embarrassment at their presence. From time to time a new grad student would come, from Toronto or Cornell, and ask who got to listen to the tapes, and my friend Jeff Tulis would shrug and say, "Just another hoplite in the Straussian Army."

There were strict hierarchies, spoken and unspoken. The Straussians of academic legend, clustering at the feet of the master, looking for secret teachings, hoping for a mark of favor, sure that they had access to Nature or the Truth, were treated a little bit like untutored rustics in the presence of civilization. Jeff, who was studying Greek, called them the *epigoni*, using the Greek word for followers and toadies. This phenomenon—the desire to be a disciple, to find a master, to form an exclusive intellectual cult—is by no means peculiar to the Straussians. I have seen it among the students of Arendt, Wolin, Habermas, and Derrida, and in less elevated places. Honey attracts flies, cats (even very clean cats) get fleas, children get head lice, and however much they might like to be rid of them, it is often a difficult enterprise.

There were lineages. There were rankings, formal and informal. But there was also a radical equality. Students and teachers addressed each other formally. I was Miss Norton to Mr. Lerner, Mr. Kass, and Mr. Bloom. This rather formal equality extended to the classroom. We read the same texts in the same way. Sometimes one professor would come to another's class. No one could argue from authority, and a lifetime of learning was subordinated to the text. No one could refer to the latest article, or "the literature," or an array of secondary sources for support. These, like all other arguments, had to be made through the text before us all. In a classroom where conventional distinctions are stripped away, other distinctions come to the fore.

Ambitious students were unleashed. They learned the pleasures of a common endeavor and the pleasures of contest. They learned to like the taste of their professors' blood. They learned, quickly enough, to be something more than students. They learned that when they succeeded most fully they would not be praised. They would be fought as rivals, they would be resented. Perhaps they would surpass their professors. They learned that the best of their professors longed for this, thinking, like Nietzsche, that "all those who go on their own way, carry my image too into the breaking day."

The *epigoni* looked for little marks of favor. Some students, there as everywhere, came looking for a master, for inclusion, for selection, for a cult. If Cropsey and Lerner were not willing to give them that, there were others. Those sought disciples as actively as disciples sought masters, though not always in the right places. Leon Kass, now in the Bush administration, once saw that I had an interest in a particular interpretation he had quoted.

The interpretation, he told me, had come from a commentary of which there were only six copies in all the world. I could look at it, he said, if I would read it in his office and under his eye, and then of course, we could discuss it together. Not all seductions are sexual. I declined the invitation, but mentioned it later to Cropsey. "Oh, do you want to read that?" he asked. Then he pulled open the bottom drawer of a file cabinet, took out a manuscript and handed it to me. If you want, you can see it, too. Later someone (no doubt one of the privileged six) published it. It is called "The Lion and the Ass."

Strauss did not teach quite as I was taught. He lectured. He had a reader, his students tell me, who would read a passage until Strauss signaled to him to stop. Then Strauss would comment on the passage. Strauss expected deference, and perhaps disciples. He demanded loyalty. He formed a school. Yet Strauss, I am told, was delighted by the (relative) equality of the American academy. In Germany one was "Herr (or Frau) Doktor Professor." In the American academy (at least its more elevated reaches) one was simply "Mr." or "Miss." In these circles, calling oneself "Dr." was simply a sign that one had not gone to a very good school.

This was the place of the Chicago Straussians: It was cold. A Chicago T-shirt reads, "The University of Chicago: Hell Does Freeze Over." Chicago students were passionate, obsessive. Each had one or two obsessions: Mayan hieroglyphics and Alban Berg, medieval romances and Marvel comics, Anselm Kiefer and string theory. They were ascetic. There wasn't much money for scholarships, and few students came from wealthy families. They worked, in bookstores and coffee shops, but more often (because the money was better) in labs, washing the dishes and feeding the rats. Late at night in quiet corners of the hospital you could hear snatches of conversation on how Tennstedt conducted Mahler, or the meaning of *dasein* in *Being and Time*. People frowned in disapproval if you wore a new pair of jeans, but they would live on ramen noodles all week to buy a good burgundy or make dinner for their friends. They were connoisseurs—of food, wine, music, baseball, and classes. Students talked incessantly about their classes, who was brilliant, who was a fraud, who was on the way to something.

An old friend of mine who went to college at Princeton came to visit me at Chicago. "At Princeton," he said, "we're well-rounded. Chicago is full of brilliant neurotics." We were flattered. Neurosis was a small price to pay for brilliance. The library was open twenty-four hours a day during the week, and you could have pizza and ribs, fried chicken and Chinese food delivered. In those days, all the deliverymen knew the address of the library. We ate there, we slept there, we had sex in the stacks. In Chicago, in my time and before, these passions combined to make what we called "the life of the mind."

As this suggests, classes were not simply classes at Chicago, or indeed anywhere where the students of Strauss or the Straussians taught. You didn't take classes to get a degree, or the credentials you needed for law school or business school. You took classes for higher and for lower—or at least more mundane—reasons: because you were obsessed with Aristotle or Machiavelli; because you were a disciple of the teacher; because the professor was here from France or Germany; because he was involved in some wild scholarly dispute; or—perversely—because the class was said to be desperately hard and only a very few people did well in it. Chicago was a place where intellectual passions ran unchecked. That passion remains strong, even among those Straussians who have left the academy. It is one of their greatest virtues.

If the Straussians were, as they are often said to be, a kind of priesthood, they would be a teaching order. Teaching has kept the Straussians alive. When major research universities were reluctant to hire Straussians (or indeed, any political theorists), liberal arts colleges did. These places, where students are taught by conversation, were hospitable to a school that regarded dialogue as perhaps the highest form of inquiry. In time (not very much time), the great universities remembered that Socrates had taught in this way, and they returned to holding it in fairly high regard.

Straussians adore their teachers. They talk about them the way young girls talk about horses and boy bands, but they listen to them. They tell stories about what movies their teachers liked—Strauss's favorite was said to be *Zulu*—and other trivialities. They tell affectionate, mocking stories about their practical incapacities, like the time Strauss and Jacob Klein went off to buy a baby present. Other stories were parables. Strauss said, or so I was told, that one should always teach as if there were one student in the class who was more intelligent than you were and another who was more virtuous.

Among the most controversial aspects of Straussian teaching is something that might seem quite obvious and sensible. For Strauss, the students of Strauss, and the Straussians, nothing is more important than the book you are reading. That book, the text, is the final authority. Students are taught to set aside what they know of the book or its author, what other people have said or written about it. Secondary sources are dispensable. Instead one is to approach the book without preconceptions, not knowing what one will find in it. This overlooks much superb scholarship and it deprives the student (at least in the early years) of the help of other scholars, but it has its virtues and advantages. Students are taught to read the text on their own. They (and the professor) are made more honest by the insistence that all claims must be supported by the text. An element of equality and common purpose enters early: all read the same text, all are held to the same standard of judgment. These practices are not peculiar to the Straussians, but they are strong in them.

The text should also, must also, be of a certain kind. The text must be what is called a "great book." Straussians don't teach comic books or fotonovellas, the *National Enquirer* or *Cosmopolitan*, as a cultural studies professor might. They don't teach the debates in Congress. They don't study treaties, laws, or the process of lawmaking. A daring one might show a film, especially if it is one of those films said to be favorite of Strauss's, like *Zulu*. A modest one might turn to Supreme Court opinions or presidential addresses.

Following these principles has made many Straussians good teachers, especially for the young, but these—like other virtues—can carry vices with them. Seeing the richness of the canon—or indeed of a single work—may persuade a student that all the knowledge of the universe can be found within a single text. Aristotle and—astonishingly—the *Federalist Papers* seem to have this effect on the susceptible. The student armed with the sacred text believes himself prepared to take on all comers. The student who believes all knowledge rests in the canon is exempted from reading anything else, and loudly presents his laziness as the inevitable entitlement of cultural superiority. These defects are not, of course, confined to students. Bellow's "no Fijian Tolstoy" is an instance of the same laziness. There is no Fijian Tolstoy, assuredly; there is also no American Hegel, no French Lao Tzu, no German Whitman, no Swedish Yehuda Amichai, but in each place there are great minds and works of beauty, grace, and richness.

Reading works regarded as great—works from the canon—stores up resources. The student who reads Plato learns not only Plato but that which is necessary to understand al Farabi, Nietzsche, and Lacan. Not only Rousseau's work but the work of Lévi-Strauss and Derrida open to the student who reads Rousseau. Marx opens to the reader of Hegel, Hegel and Aquinas open to the reader of Aristotle. Each work gives entrée not only to one man's work but to many. For this reason many of us—poststructuralists as well as Straussians, liberals, and Marxists—believe that teaching great works is a good idea.

For some, however, there is more at stake. One should teach not simply great works but a canon. A canon in this sense is not simply a list of especially influential, well-regarded, and fundamentally valuable works. Nor is it simply a way in to broader fields of inquiry. Instead, the canon is something more—and so, something less. For these people, the canon is a heritage, a legacy, a set of sacred texts preserving the collective wisdom vouchsafed to a particular people, or to a civilization.

This teaching does not do justice to the works it praises. Teaching the canon is reduced to a form of ancestor worship. Works that were once thought great as thought, great as philosophy, not bound by space and time, are now presented as great simply because they are ours. Works once thought to speak across great distances now speak only to the ear of a countryman. Works once thought to have value beyond their time and place, to speak in some sense to anyone and everyone, become a currency that circulates only within certain boundaries. To attach an ethnic or cultural title to these texts diminishes them. They do not remain diminished. A clever, or merely inquisitive, student will observe that these supposedly ancestral texts are alien: written by idol-worshiping heathens, barbarians from the back of beyond, or others with debts to our supposed cultural antagonists. In seeing that the text is alien, they join a larger community.

There are more dangerous vices in these virtues. Too often, students see the richness of the text in the hand of the one who holds it out to them, hear the words of writers long dead from the mouth of their teacher. The beauty of a new mind, the sight of another's pleasure, the memory of one's own learning, can deceive a teacher into desire. Any responsible teacher must have sufficient discipline to recognize and reject this desire. There are a few who prey on—or fall prey to—that diverted desire. More often (but not much better) the teacher draws students around him. These students want a master, this teacher wants disciples. Straussians, who respect their teachers so profoundly, may be especially vulnerable to these dangers.

Straussians know who each other's teachers are, who went to school with whom, and whom they taught in turn. One knows many of the books they have read, the stories they know, the questions they might ask. They have catchphrases, as most academic schools do, and they are contrarian. They talk of "reason and revelation," "the one and the many," "Ancients and Moderns." When political science pretended to have no interest in morals, a Straussian would ask whether it was just, whether it was right, whether it "belonged to the good." When academics talked about culture, Straussians would talk about nature. They tell one another stories: about Strauss and about the great philosophers. Many of these are taken from the canon: stories about how

Socrates walked around Athens barefoot, about Machiavelli washing and changing his clothes to spend his nights in the company of Livy, about Hegel writing to support his mistress, and Nietzsche throwing his arms around a beaten cart horse. They read the same books over and over: Plato's *Apology*, the *Crito*, and the *Symposium*; Aristotle (the *Ethics*, not the *Politics*); Thucydides, Machiavelli, the *Federalist Papers*, Tocqueville.

In this book, I will tell you how the teachings of Leo Strauss made their way from the quiet corners of classrooms and dorms, bookstores and labs, into the precincts of power, and what became of them when they came there.

3 *Decline into the West*

Leo Strauss entered the American academy from a particular place, in a particular time, and in particular company. Among the most important figures in this intellectual company are Martin Heidegger, Hannah Arendt, and Carl Schmitt. Arendt and Strauss were of the same place and time, and in many respects (though this will astonish and appall their more zealous adherents) the same intellectual tastes. They emerged from the same intellectual environment. They were German Jews, educated in the German universities of the 1920s and 1930s. The German academy had betrayed them, yet they were very much of it.

For Strauss, for Arendt, the shadow had fallen on Europe. The rise and fall of Nazism had been followed by another totalitarianism. The threat of the Soviet Union was not merely the threat of totalitarianism, it was the threat of the East: of Oriental despotism and the Asiatic cast of mind, of custom, superstition, and cruelty. Reason had fled with the refugees to America. America was, as Hegel had famously written, the evening land, beyond the horizon, the place of the future, a land outside history. Yet, as Strauss recalled in *The City and Man*, the owl of Minerva flies at twilight. Perhaps in the failing light of the evening land, philosophy might again take flight.

This is the sentiment with which Bloom concluded *The Closing of the American Mind*. "This is the American moment in world history," he wrote, and "the fate of philosophy in the world has devolved upon our universities." Democracy, republicanism, had a home in America. Americans had never known monarchy. They were, as Tocqueville wrote, born equal, and born to equality. They were born in a republic, and born for democracy. Their habits, their expectations, their prejudices were democratic. They were at home in the republic. Fascism and communism, especially in their totalitarian forms, were alien to Americans. They were not only democrats, they were American democrats: suspicious of governmental authority, accustomed to the power that had no center. For them power was diffused among the states, one found it among aldermen and mayors as well as senators and presidents, in school boards as well as senate hearings. Democracy might prosper here as it could not in Athens. It was an American animal, and it had been domesticated.

Philosophy was another matter. Europeans, and for that matter, Asians and Middle Easterners, Africans and Latin Americans, have looked at America and judged it a country hostile not only to philosophy but to intellectual life. Americans often pride themselves on their anti-intellectualism. Just yesterday I read an article about a small Texas town that, when reproached for declining intellectual standards, seized for itself the proud title of "dumb clods." Mencken castigated the American "booboisie."

Strauss was a refugee, part of the University in Exile. The Straussians belong, with the students of Arendt, to the revival of philosophy in exile, the renaissance of political theory in America. Strauss and Arendt were alike in their tastes and ties, their intellectual genealogies, and their historical experiences. They were alike in what they had learned, whom they had studied, and how it had served them. Both had been impressed by Heidegger. Both regarded Heidegger as a philosopher of unquestioned brilliance. Both had been, in some sense, betrayed by him. The story of the relation of these three is often cast in terms of love.

Hannah Arendt had been Heidegger's lover as well as his student. Heidegger's accommodation with the Nazis was thus a betrayal of a student and a lover—a private as well as a political betrayal. Strauss and Arendt had known each other in Germany. Once in the United States, they became associated (as they had in Germany) with different politics and different philosophic schools. This would seem to be enough to explain the hostility between them, but it hasn't been adequate for biographers and academic gossips. Both groups tell the same story, with variations. Strauss courted Arendt, the story goes, and she rejected him.

One version has her reject him because he was not Zionist enough, another because he had initially admired Hitler, a third because of his conservatism. None is reliable, but all capture the peculiar mix of affinity and animus that linked these two immigrant philosophers: Whatever separated Strauss and Arendt, the stories tell us, it was a romance gone wrong.

Arendt and Strauss seem in important respects to belong together, as political philosophers, as students of Heidegger, as Jews, as exiles, as refugees in a foreign land. They were alike in their regard for the ancient philosophy, especially that of the Greeks, and in their common ambivalence to their adopted country. They were both thoroughly European in their dismissal of the African and Asian elements of American culture. They both distrusted the politics and culture of what they would call the masses, what others might call the people. Both did well in their new country, were welcomed, recognized, praised. Each attracted a group of students and won the attention of intellectuals. They were, however, very much at odds. The students of Strauss scorned Arendt, the admirers of Arendt shunned Strauss and scorned the Straussians. Their romance gone wrong shaped both politics and philosophy in America.

In 1932, as the shadow descended on Europe, Strauss made a series of comments on a text by Carl Schmitt. The text was *The Concept of the Political*. Schmitt was to become the leading jurist of the Third Reich. Before that, he wrote a letter recommending Leo Strauss for the fellowship that would enable him to make his way out of Germany and make a life, and a scholarly career, in England and America. When we read these notes, we can see shadows on the page: the shadow of what is to come, and the indistinct shapes of two men, Catholic and Jew, one who will rise only to fall, and one who will fall only to rise. The man of the faith, the jurist of the Prussian State Council, meets the reasoning son of the covenant. The one empowered by the law of man meets the one whose birth and faith make him the law's prey. Strauss found a home in exile. Schmitt remained in Germany, only to find after the war that home had become an exile.

The political, Schmitt argued, was a category, a concept, separate from the moral, the economic, and the aesthetic. Morality was defined by the opposition of good and evil, the economic by the opposition of profit and loss, the aesthetic by the opposition of the beautiful and the ugly. The political was defined by the relation between friend and enemy. This relation overshadowed the others, however, for the relation of friend and enemy went to the heart of existence. The enemy presented the threat of death, of annihilation, not merely to a person, but to the nation, and the nation's form of life. Because that threat could arise in the realm of morality, or economics, or even aesthetics, any of these realms could become political. Modernity, especially modern liberalism, had lost sight of the distinct character of these realms. For modern liberals, Schmitt argued, everything became a social question, and the fundamental distinctions of politics were hidden.

Arendt and Strauss agreed in their view of the importance of the political. Schmitt had shaped the term for each of them. Strauss gave *The Concept of the Political* a more than sympathetic reading. Strauss, Schmitt believed, had understood him better than any other man, better, perhaps, than he understood himself. He had incorporated Strauss's understanding into his work. Strauss was to incorporate elements of Schmitt's work in his own critique of liberalism. Arendt's use of "the political" echoes in the writings of her students and colleagues.

Arendt accepted Schmitt's insistence on recognizing the political as a distinct realm. She shared Schmitt's anxiety that the social had become a category that swallowed up all others. She refused, however, the notion that aspects of the social realm— economics, for example—might become political. Arendt divided the world into the political and the social. The social was not political and should not be made so. The social was the realm of the private. Politics was public. The preservation of privacy, of the integrity of private life, depended on keeping the social free of politics. The preservation of the transcendent character of politics, the integrity of the light-filled public realm, depended on keeping the social out of politics.

For Arendt, the separation of the political and the social remains requisite to republics. A good, healthy politics depends on keeping each in its place. Arendt lived, however, in an America that had begun to question the distinction between public and private. The civil rights movement brought these questions to the fore. Arendt's essay "Reflections on Little Rock" showed the consequences of her position. Segregation was social, Arendt argued, and should not be addressed by political means. Sending federal troops to Little Rock would rupture the boundary between the political and the social and place the republic in danger. One could—and should—repeal laws against miscegenation, but one should not integrate schools. Arendt's failure to recognize the possibility of particular "social" issues becoming political underlay her failure to recognize that race was a political issue in the United States. It led her to contemptuously dismiss the politics of black pride in America, and the importance of the nonaligned movement, the Third World, in global politics.

Strauss had underlined the importance of recognizing the potentially political character of all economic, moral, and aesthetic disputes, but this seems to have left his students no better equipped to deal with these issues and movements. Initially they tended to dismiss arguments about politics in art, aesthetics, popular culture, and ordinary life. Like the students of Arendt— and most American liberals—they insisted that black power and feminism were social rather than political. Later they recognized the political character of debates over culture and simply deplored their direction. The latter recognition followed Strauss and Schmitt. The students of Strauss learned that the personal— the aesthetic, the moral, the economic, the cultural—could be political. The long hair and unconventional clothing of the counterculture, the symbolic burning of flags and bras and draft cards, were acts that had become political. The students of

Strauss wasted no time insisting upon the social rather than political character of these actions; they were well prepared to recognize as politics what had once appeared as merely social disputes. While the students of Arendt saw these conflicts as misplaced and urged people to return them to their proper (social) sphere, the Straussians were ready to meet their enemies on common ground. Recognizing that culture had become the terrain of politics, they prepared to fight the culture wars.

The Straussians looked forward, but Strauss looked backward, over his shoulder at an abandoned Europe. For Strauss and Arendt—and many after them—all political events were seen in relation to the rise and fall of Nazi Germany. Events in Europe had not merely shaped their understanding of politics, they had provided the model for understanding all politics, everywhere. Memory overlay their reading of politics.

The children of Heidegger brought to America the hope that politics and philosophy might be found not in the person of the philosopher-king but in the democracy. This hope (not so very differently expressed) was instilled by Strauss and Arendt into their (not so very different) students. Out of it came Sheldon Wolin's *Politics and Vision,* as well as Leo Strauss's *Natural Right and History.* The revival of political philosophy was allied to a revival of politics.

Those who had sent political philosophy into exile thought that politics could be a science. Political scientists would operate like meteorologists: predicting the political climate. Debates about justice, about right, about the rise of national socialism, the dropping of the atomic bomb, the civil rights movement, and the war in Vietnam were "value-laden," and the "scientists" scorned them. Students did not. They looked to their world as students often look, with a passionate desire to understand the operation of power, a passionate desire to see power allied with right. The study of politics involved, they saw, more than measurement. They found that political theory, political philosophy, spoke directly to the politics they saw. The hordes of impassioned students went variously from Strauss to Edward Shils or Bruno Bettleheim or Joseph Cropsey; from Arendt to Sheldon Wolin or Herbert Marcuse. Some went from one way of thinking to others, taking with them a passion for learning, for philosophy, for the political.

All of those involved in the revival of political theory looked at a political science with the politics ostentatiously excised, and found it wanting. Strauss himself offered a critical appraisal of the discipline's self-mutilation. His essay became the center of a book of essays critical of political science. The book, edited by Herbert Storing, was entitled *Essays in the Scientific Study of Politics.* Twenty years later, older Straussian students were to call it "the hate book." The book was a collection of essays critical of major figures in political science. Judgments were harsh, and worse, they were occasionally witty. The reviews (at least from the point of view of the professors attacked) were often worse. Sheldon Wolin criticized the book for attacking "pipsqueaks," prompting one of the professors to respond that he preferred his Straussian enemies to his defenders.

The hate book might seem to explain, in part, the rough reception many Straussians received in the academy. It probably doesn't. Political science has never been friendly to political theory. In those years, political science was often unfriendly to politics as well. Political scientists searched desperately for some aspect of politics that could be studied scientifically, without the passionate conviction people bring to politics. They wanted (some still want) a politics without good and evil, right and wrong, honor and dishonor, praise and blame. They wanted (some still want) politics analytically separated from the actions of the powerful and the lives of the ordinary. They wanted, in short, no politics worth studying, and they very nearly got it. Politics, however, could not be closed out of the academy for long. American life had become profoundly—and, what is more, consciously—political. The Cold War, the arms race, the civil rights movement, and the war in Vietnam brought politics into every kitchen and dining room in America. When marchers filled the streets, politics seemed to come back to the academy. Politics had never really left.

The students of Strauss (and the students of the students of Strauss) who now walk the corridors of power walked a different set of corridors in the sixties and seventies. In Chicago some of them formed what my professors called "Straussian truth squads." They constituted themselves as bands of intellectual vigilantes, entering the classrooms of professors they disliked or distrusted, asking questions not to hear the answers but as a form of disruption and intimidation. Those professors who held to the Weberian tenet that a professor "ought not to carry a marshal's baton in his rucksack" were asked about their values and their politics. Professors who had less respect for Leo Strauss than for political theory were read quotations from *Natural Right and History*. The behaviorists (for the most part, true believers themselves) were mocked for their lack of learning and castigated for their pretensions to ethical neutrality. Their claim that they were engaged in science, and so apart from—and above—politics, sounded all too close to the claims of Nazi scientists.

The Straussian truth squads saw themselves as following in the footsteps of Socrates, acting as a gadfly. Others saw them as intellectual brownshirts, engaged in a campaign of deliberate intimidation. The truth squads saw themselves as speaking truth to power, reviving philosophy in the New World. Their targets saw them as attempting to silence, through harassment and intimidation, all who disagreed with them. I learned about the Straussian truth squads from Strauss's old enemies, and from his students. No one defended them. The fullest and most critical account came, when I asked, from Joseph Cropsey. Strauss, however, does not appear to have discouraged the truth squads. On the contrary, Strauss seems to have been a zealous participant in the partisan politics of his department, his university, and the American academy. At the University of Chicago he tried to establish complete control over the department, and very nearly succeeded. Aided by a devoted departmental secretary, he directed financial aid to the students he preferred and tried to control hiring in the department.

Conservatives who bewail the presence of politics in the academy forget how much of that politics is conservative, and how furiously it is pursued. The Straussian truth squads who roamed the halls of Chicago mocking behaviorists, calling on their professors to ask questions not only about facts but about values, who rejected the claims of science to ethical neutrality, who sought an orthodox unity in the pursuit of the good were not far in their aims, their lineage, or their teaching, from the students of Berkeley, Columbia, and Cornell. The students of Arendt who read *Crises of the Republic* were not so very different in their reactions from the students who read *Natural Right and History*. They saw the republic in danger. They saw hope in the principles of the revolution, in the words of the Declaration of Independence. They hoped that those principles could be revived. They suspected that the principles alone would not be quite enough.

Each of these campuses—Berkeley, Columbia, Chicago, and Cornell—became a battleground in the 1960s and 1970s. Each was the site of demonstrations against the war in Vietnam. Each saw the struggles and felt the repercussions of the civil rights movement. On each campus debate moved from the classroom to the street and back again. These struggles led to broader movements: free speech, black power, feminism. Each campus felt, to varying degrees, the conservative backlash. At each university, national and international controversies took on local form.

In Chicago some students joined the large and active chapter of Students for a Democratic Society. Students from the university demonstrated with the Yippies during the Democratic Convention of 1968. There were marches and demonstrations in Hyde Park, on the university's campus, as well. The university, often at odds with the city, refused to let the police on campus and put up bail for many arrested students. One struggle was contained, another struggled to be born, as alienated conservatives took their partisanship to the classroom.

Berkeley became a staging ground for movement after movement: free speech, and (with the help of Oakland) black power and the Black Panthers, hippies, and an emerging environmental politics. Berkeley—indeed, the entire state of California—seemed to be playing on a larger stage, conscious that local struggles had historic importance, contending over the shape of the world they were making. At Cornell, as at Columbia, demonstrations turned violent and divided the university against itself.

There were a number of Straussians at Cornell in the time of the revolt: Allan Bloom, who taught many of the neoconservatives; Abram Shulsky, who went from one intelligence community to another; Walter Berns, the teacher of conservative jurists; Donald Kagan, who made Thucydides the architect of American empire. The events at Cornell altered their lives. Allan Bloom's life was, he thought, divided in two, altering his relation to politics and to philosophy. Because these events altered their worlds, they altered those of their students. Because these men and their students came to power, they have altered our world as well. The explosions at Cornell sent shock waves through the academy and—slowly and inexorably—through the nation. Perhaps the shock waves from that explosion are shaking Iraq.

Donald Downs has written a detailed account of these events in *Cornell '69*. I found it invaluable and recommend it to you, though I disagree with Don about the meaning of these events. In the early 1960s Cornell had made a commitment to the practice and principles of the civil rights movement, finding and admitting African-American students. The university, to its credit, admitted enough black students that they could no longer be seen simply as the exemplary exception. They were a presence on the campus, large enough that Cornell was obliged to confront the questions of race in America not as a problem for one or two individuals but as the nation did: as questions confronting us all. Once, acts of discrimination at the university could be addressed as individual acts of bigotry or rudeness or dismissed as the effects of personal sensitivity. The presence of more African Americans forced Cornell to confront discrimination as a political and national rather than as a personal and social problem.

Cornell was riven, as many campuses were, by the expanding war in Vietnam, resistance to the draft, and the emergence of Students for a Democratic Society and other militant student organizations. Like other campuses in that time, it held students whose imaginations had been fired by the civil rights movement. By 1969, after the assassinations of John Kennedy, Bobby Kennedy, and Martin Luther King, it held the angry and disillusioned with the romantic and hopeful. By 1969 people had recognized that the great reforms of the civil rights movement were not a triumphant culmination but the beginning of a long, burdensome struggle.

Professors and administrators at the university were prepared to deal with the racist remark in class or even the assaults by students on students. They were prepared to ask African-American students into the academy. All hoped to make African Americans more academic. Far fewer were prepared to make the academy more African American. Most, professors and students alike, considered discrimination a matter of conflicts between individuals or—for the more discerning—discrimination in admissions. They were unprepared for the possibility that African Americans might remake the academy they entered: the arrangement of dorms and dining halls, the content of colleges and the curriculum. Those already within the universities thought they knew what education was, what learning meant. They were unprepared for the possibility that the meaning of education would broaden as African Americans entered the university. African Americans were to enter the university, and the university was to remain unchanged. As Walter Berns said in his resignation speech, "We had too good a world; it couldn't last."

The Straussians who found themselves in the midst of a student revolt at Cornell had found Cornell a very good world, if not a paradise. Bloom was a shopkeeper's son from Indianapolis. For Bloom, for Donald Kagan (who was to found his own academic lineage), for Werner Dannhauser, becoming a professor and entering the once-closed world of the Ivy League were political as well as personal triumphs. Dannhauser recalled Bloom saying to him, "You know what they're saying about us two Jewboys in the Ivy League? There goes theory at Cornell—that's what they're saying." Perhaps Bloom was simply warding off the evil eye. Cornell had opened its doors to him, to Dannhauser, and to many others. They were applauded there. Their own inclusion was fresh and new, and they found it hard to recognize that anyone remained outside.

All parties recognized that the battle at Cornell was a battle for the university, for the academy. For African-American students and their white allies, the struggle was for a more fundamental form of integration. They saw that Berns's "too good a world" was not good enough. For those in what Downs calls the "counter revolt," the response to African-American student demands was a response to armed intimidation. They saw themselves defending, past its fall, the lost world of openness and academic freedom.

The commitment of Bloom, Berns, Dannhauser, Shulsky, and the other "counter-revolutionaries" to academic freedom is marred by their past and future tolerance of tactics of intimidation on the right, by their employment of such tactics at Cornell, and by their treatment of another professor of political science, Clinton Rossiter. All the Straussians knew, and some had participated in, the truth squads at Chicago. Some, Bloom notably among them, later endorsed and participated in a politics of censorship and intimidation. Rossiter had voted first for the university to stand fast in its resistance to African-American student demands, then changed his vote to support a policy of accommodation. Perhaps Rossiter's change of vote was weakness, perhaps it was a principled change of heart, perhaps it was pandering. His former allies met it with contempt. They shunned him in private and turned their backs on him in public A commitment to academic freedom does not require that one like or respect one's colleagues. But that commitment, and praise of an open university, sit badly with an unrelenting and totalitarian enforcement of orthodoxy in opinion. Rossiter haunted their offices asking for forgiveness. One of them, a Straussian, responded, "Clinton, I am a hard man. And when I decide no longer to have anything to do with a person, he's dead as far as I am concerned." Rossiter was dead within a year. He committed suicide.

The parties to these conflicts, and the consequences of the conflicts themselves, altered as the participants grew older, moved, and found themselves in other places, in another time, with a different set of political struggles. Carey McWilliams, once a leader of the free speech movement at Berkeley, grew closer to the Straussians in politics and method. Paul Wolfowitz, advancing the war in Iraq, condemned the war in Vietnam. Michael Zuckert, a fellow student of Wolfowitz's, took to the streets to protest the war in Iraq. People chose different paths to the same ends, changed their minds and their politics, altered their tactics and strategies.

There were other changes. Those who came to school after African Americans had begun to alter the meaning of the university came into another world. For us, an ordinary education offered not only knowledge of Europe but knowledge of Africa and Asia. Studying American politics meant reading not only Tocqueville's *Democracy in America* and the *Federalist Papers*. We read Du Bois's *The Souls of Black Folk* and Fanon's *Wretched of the Earth*. We took those understandings into our minds, and often into our hearts. Many of us, professors now, were white suburban children then. We watched television. We saw the fire hoses in the streets of Birmingham, sweeping black bodies away in torrents. We looked into the open mouths of Bull Connor's German shepherds as he sent them to attack unarmed marchers. Tocqueville and Publius would not have been enough for us. The demands of African Americans were not, as Arendt had thought, merely "self-interested." They were for us. The students at Cornell led to changes not only at Cornell but throughout the American academy. Because of these changes, we could read Du Bois as well as Tocqueville, Beard, and Hartz. We could study with John Hope Franklin and St. Clair Drake. We could become, we hoped, more African American.

Don Downs sees Cornell of 1969 as a tragic confrontation between academic freedom and social justice. This is, I think, how Bloom and his allies saw it. They saw demands for racial justice in tragic and inexorable conflict with academic freedom. They believed that the African Americans who occupied Willard Straight Hall and demanded black studies were silencing them, violating their freedom to teach as they chose. They thought the academy they had had was too good to last because it had been good to them. Taking to the streets seemed radically opposed to the quiet philosophy of the Athenian academy they reverenced. I am not sure it was. Socrates sauntered through Athens challenging the learned and the powerful, the rich and the skilled, trailing obstreperous (and often spoiled) students in his wake. Plato and Aristotle concerned themselves very little with freedom. Justice stands at the center of the *Republic*, the *Politics*, and the *Ethics*. The old imperative "The unexamined life is not worth living" demanded attention to African-American history and politics more insistently than the students could. Bloom and the other Cornell Straussians saw the Athenian moment become real only to find it rowdier than they had expected.

Americans, unlike the Athenians, have had more confidence that freedom and justice could be reconciled. They worked hand in hand at Cornell. For those of us who came after 1969, the lesson of Cornell may be that academic freedom and racial justice were not opposed but allied. The students' demands brought more— and more learned—professors into the academy: white as well as black. An academy that was more nearly just made academic freedom not merely an ideal but an experience for African—and so for all—Americans. An academy that discriminates is not a paradise of academic freedom for anybody. A little thought about race and justice worked to free American colleges and universities from the burdens of discrimination: not only in the dorms but in the classrooms, not only in who could be admitted but in what could be taught. Bloom wrote: "The most successful tyranny is not the one that uses force to assure uniformity, but the one that removes awareness of other possibilities." For many years the universities had been—perhaps blissfully—unaware of the possibilities of scholarship. Those who believed the old order had been too good to last could not always see the world that opened before them. They mourned the world they had lost. Tocqueville mourned the lost world of the aristocracy, but he saw the virtues of the new. The opening democratic world seemed barren and hard to him, "but it is more just, and in its justice lies its greatness and beauty." The beauty of that world was hidden from Bloom and his colleagues. They could not see justice in democracy.

Strauss and Arendt had, in Ludwig Wittgenstein's phrase, a family resemblance. They instilled in their students a common passion for politics and philosophy. Though their students and disciples often found themselves at odds or even on opposite sides of the barricades, they too bore traces of that familial resemblance. Their parents were the children of Heidegger. We who know that in philosophy, if not in politics, the children kill the fathers should not be surprised to find Heidegger's children insisting on the presence of philosophy in politics. They may have felt that Heidegger's shameful insistence on the capacity of philosophy to distance itself from politics left them something to repair.

Strauss and Arendt had succeeded this far: philosophy and the study of the political returned to the American academy, and with a vengeance.

4   *Closing the American Mind*

Allan Bloom experienced Cornell as a profound defeat, but he made it the occasion for a later victory. He wrote a book, inspired by his tribulations at Cornell, called *The Closing of the American Mind*. The book was that rare thing in academic circles, a popular success and a publishing phenomenon. It climbed to the top of the bestseller lists in 1987 and remained there. In subsequent editions it went on to sell more than a million copies.

Bloom's *Closing of the American Mind* announced the conservative position in the emergent cultural wars. Bloom's polemic against undergraduate education, rock music, the fall of romance, and the rise of sexuality captured the public imagination. Talk show hosts and journalists hailed the book. People talked about it in classes and coffee shops. The more philosophic Straussians ignored the book or deprecated it quietly. In it Bloom had committed half the sins in the philosophic canon. The book was meretricious, not merely speaking but pandering to the vulgar. Cavalier polemic had taken the place of scholarship. Philosophy deferred to convention. Bloom's loud suits and raucous manner, his turning from philosophy, his self-indulgence, his squandering of ability took literary form in it. The simply political Straussians rejoiced. They had a market. They had a public voice. Their triumph was all the richer for being double. They had won a battle against what they had learned to call political correctness. They had won a fame and voice their more philosophic colleagues lacked. The philosophic might continue their patronizing, but the political Straussians would have the power.

Bloom, far more than Strauss, has shaped the Straussians who govern in America. Bloom taught both the most powerful and the most vociferously ideological of the Straussians. The most conspicuous of the Straussians in the Reagan and the two Bush administrations have ties to Allan Bloom. Bloom prided himself on his connections to power, and as his students acquired it, he boasted of the connection. After Bloom's death, his friend Saul Bellow wrote a roman à clef, *Ravelstein*, with Bloom as the protagonist. One of the most famous episodes (at least among Straussians) in the book comes when Ravelstein (Bloom) receives a phone call from a government official (Wolfowitz) giving him advance notice of a military action. It says something about Bloom and something about Wolfowitz that most Straussians believe the incident to be a fictional gift from Bellow to Bloom, a moment of posthumous wish fulfillment.

Paul Wolfowitz, in an interview in *Vanity Fair*, insists that talk of a Straussian cabal is "absurd." He, for example, "took two courses with Leo Strauss." This is a little disingenuous, for if he ate lightly of the main dish, there were others on the table. He does tell the interviewer, albeit obliquely, that he studied with Allan Bloom, and that he lived in the college house Bloom mastered. For any Straussian, the mention of Telluride House signals a more intense relation with Allan Bloom. At Telluride House, Wolfowitz turned from mathematics to political theory, and to Bloom's Strauss.

The circle at Telluride House then, and for some years later, revolved around Allan Bloom. Bloom lived in the house. Other students regarded the circle as a Straussian cult. Other Straussians, even at Cornell, looked askance at the intensity of the master-disciple relation, calling Bloom's students "the blossoms." Telluride had the hothouse atmosphere of cultic discipleship and dissident conservatism. Bloom held his students to a conservative orthodoxy. He also held them in a particularly intense form of discipleship.

Years later, after Bloom's death, a Straussian colleague, Werner

Dannhauser, recalled the anger and disillusionment he and Bloom had experienced at Cornell. "He was cut to the quick by those who proudly proclaimed that teaching was primarily a power relation. He hit back hard." Why should Bloom have been "cut to the quick" by so innocuous a statement? Bloom's teacher, Leo Strauss, expected the degree of deference that German professors before the war demanded of their students, and a little more. They were expected to bow a little and pick up the dry cleaning. Strauss called his students "my puppies." Bloom himself liked to play little games with his puppies. "He was tossing pennies down the hall, and his students were scurrying to pick them up off the floor," my friend Peter Agree told me. "He was laughing."

Bloom taught enormous classes at Cornell, lecturing to four hundred or five hundred students in a class. He was by all accounts a spellbinding lecturer. People who heard his lectures tell me that they were fascinating, humorous, and astonishingly dramatic. Students applauded each class as if it were a theatrical performance. Perhaps it was. Bloom chain-smoked through each class, using the cigarette in artful gestures, pausing in the middle of a sentence to light a cigarette, drawing the moment out. He was dramatic in word and gesture, and he held his audience of students enthralled. He rarely spoke of politics in class in those days.

Things changed after Cornell. At Chicago there were no large classes, no applause. There were small seminars of less-appreciative students. Politics was unavoidable in his classes. Before I left Chicago, I sat in on a course he offered on Rousseau. Bloom gave extended reviews of a Susan Brownmiller book, *Against Our Will*, a book then some years old. He animadverted at length on the state of American political culture. I waited in vain for Rousseau. Chicago students, even Chicago Straussians, were not accustomed to the privileging of politics over philosophy in class. Nor did they expect the demands for attention and loyalty that Bloom made of his students. People left the classes. There were shouting matches. Bloom refused to grade the papers of a student who had "listened to other professors." There were rumors, which the terms of Bloom's appointment seemed to confirm, that he had been refused by the Political Science Department. Bloom settled in at Chicago, but the applause that had followed him at Cornell never returned.

Success did. As *The Closing of the American Mind* became a literary phenomenon, winning a popular following, Bloom's friends celebrated, seeing the book's celebrity as a vindication. Dannhauser recalled that he "delighted in delighting Allan with stories of its reception in Ithaca." In Chicago the book's celebrity must have done something to overcome rejection by Leo Strauss and a muted reception on his return. If the classes at Chicago didn't applaud, the audience on *Oprah* might. If Bloom lacked the regard of his more eminent colleagues, he had the friendship and praise of the novelist Saul Bellow. If Strauss had sent him away, he had done what Strauss had not done, perhaps could not do.

Success in public was shadowed in the academy and in private. Bloom's assumption of a posture of moral outrage was daring and—at least publicly—successful. The targets of Bloom's attack were too kind, too scrupulous, or perhaps too puritanical to say in print what Bloom's colleagues, friends, and students readily acknowledged. The defender of youthful innocence, family values, and traditional morality was a homosexual—and not just any homosexual, either. If Bloom's students were to be trusted, Bloom's antics gave new meaning to the term "transgression." The rumors of houseboys in sexual servitude, the evident flirtations with students, Bloom's flamboyantly queenly manner made *The Closing of the American Mind* read as high hypocrisy and awakened the old charges of secret teachings, now coupled with perverse practices. Once, in the dining room of the Institute for Advanced Study at Princeton, another political theorist asked me, "Isn't the secret teaching of the Straussians homosexuality?" I laughed, in part because Bloom's Cornell had been the site of a particularly ugly scandal involving sexual harassment—of women. These acts had, however, been eclipsed by the persistent rumors of homosexual rites and rituals among the Straussians: of orgiastic toga parties and gay little reenactments of the Symposium. These rumors were enhanced by Bellow's *Ravelstein*. Despite the recurrent rumors—even among Straussians and their sympathizers—I don't believe the toga parties.

What the rumors captured was sex rather than sexuality, the determined joining of men and the exclusion of women. Here the conservative values (venerated in public, disdained in private) of Allan Bloom met the modernist misogyny of Bellow on common ground. Feminism, or any of its weak sisters—women in the academy, women in the classroom, women in the workplace, women novelists—were to be disdained. Women appeared in this world, but always married, and one was always reminded, quietly, politely, that after all one knew they weren't really very good.

In its student form this had certain ironies. Tiny little men with rounded shoulders would lean back in their chairs and declare that Nature had made men superior to women. Larger, softer men, with soft white hands that never held a gun or changed a tire, delivered disquisitions on manliness. They were stronger, they were smarter, and Aristotle had said so. This may not have been entirely successful in warding off the evil eye of sexual rejection, but it seemed to furnish some consolation. There was the more troubling fact that women could read. There were those women among the students who surpassed the men easily. When they were given grades, and the rankings, and the scholarships, the male students might say, "Cropsey likes women better" or (much later): "It's affirmative action." When they read, all but the most stupid fell silent. What attracted these women? Perhaps the victory in that silence. More probably, it was beauty of the text, the opening of the door into theory. There was also then, as there is still, the dangerous discourse of the exception. You might be the exception. You might be Diotima. There were gifted women in Bloom's time. Bloom's students tell me that they filled him with terror.

There were, in short, no secret sexual teachings. The model of the secret teaching came, however, to govern the politics of sex and race. In each case here was to be a public salutary teaching, behind it an acknowledgment of an unspeakable truth. The appointments of Clarence Thomas, Colin Powell, and Condoleezza Rice declare equality, profess a commitment to a colorblind society, but power is diverted from Thomas to Scalia, from Rice and Powell to Rumsfeld and Wolfowitz.

This is the strategy of the best administrations. This is statecraft. Carnes Lord writes in *The Modern Prince* that leadership is threatened by equality. The "egalitarian turn in world history marked by the American and French Revolutions," the demise of slavery, the rise of "the common man" established a "trajectory," a "trend." "Today's political movements on behalf of the rights of minorities and women continue this trend, while radicalizing it in significant ways." Feminism has questioned "traditional male leadership," and though the feminist view is (we are told reassuringly) "almost certainly not widely shared," it has nevertheless encouraged effeminacy in democratic politics and suppressed the manly qualities of democratic leaders. Unlike many American conservatives, Lord can't find a good word to say about the redoubtable Maggie Thatcher, who possessed in abundance such "traditionally manly qualities as competitiveness, aggression, or for that matter, the ability to command." On the contrary, Thatcher is castigated for being too harsh, too demanding; for humiliating men. Manliness, and cultural deference to manliness, must be recovered.

Lord's account is carefully phrased, and very telling. The problem lies not only with women but with "today's political movements on behalf of minorities." These are, however, carefully dropped. The modern prince must be content with a word in the ear, for the modern counselor is too politic to belabor the costs of civil rights. Nor is Lord eager to go after concerns of class. He is reluctant to say what the careful reader will notice soon enough: that leaders should be men drawn from the ranks of traditional elites.

Bloom's account has none of this reluctance. Throughout *The Closing of the American Mind*, Bloom longs for a lost world of hierarchy and exclusion. From time to time, Bloom becomes a pretender to the aristocracy, reminding us that critiques of the bourgeoisie came from the right as well as the left as he inveighs against American bourgeois culture. Bloom's criticism of the bourgeoisie is confounded with a critique of American sexuality. American students are "flat-souled." Their world is "devoid of ideals" and "unadorned by imagination.... This flat soul is what the sexual wisdom of our time conspires to make universal." They lack the erotic, they lack longing. Yet as Bloom inveighs against their absence of erotic longing, a curious transformation occurs. Bloom turns to that "great expert on the fate of longing," Gustave Flaubert, drawing from *Madame Bovary* the longest quotation in his text. The passage describes how Emma Bovary sees a debauched and once-tyrannical old man, deaf and stuttering, eating from a full plate as "drops of gravy trickle from his mouth." Bloom writes: "Others see only a repulsive old man, but Emma sees the *ancien régime*." Flaubert was more ambivalent, and more discerning. Bloom sees only through Emma's eyes, but Flaubert can take our gaze a little farther. When Emma sees the ancien régime, she may see a man who "lived at court and slept in the bed of queens," but we see, with Flaubert, a repulsive slavering old lecher, the decay of tyranny into imbecility.

Flaubert also gives us some insight into Bloom's desire. Desire has been transformed, in this paragraph, from an erotics of sex to an erotics of status. Like the author of a Regency romance, Bloom claims to be telling us a story about sex, but gives us instead a story about money. As any reader of romances can tell you, what happens in a romance is not simply a story of love but a story of social advancement. Heroines enter the narrative poor and leave rich, they enter as commoners and leave as countesses. Danielle Steel has, if I understand the form correctly, removed the middle-man and given us simply narratives in which a poor woman becomes rich—very rich—and occasionally powerful.

The fantasy of the romance novel is the fantasy of the exception. The class system, the peerage, the ranks of the nobility remain intact. The poor heroine becomes an unexpected heiress, the plain heroine turns out to be really beautiful, the impoverished gentlewoman the beloved of a baronet or a billionaire. Nothing has changed, except exclusion. The pleasure of the heroine's triumph depends on the institutions that excluded her remaining intact. So it is for Bloom. The world he longs for is one in which all the old exclusions remain intact, but he is outside no longer.

The Closing of the American Mind offers a series of fantastic wishes. Bloom wishes for a world without women—or, rather, a world in which women stay behind the scenes, making dinner, making a home, out of sight, and most emphatically out of mind. In this world there are no terrifying women scholars. The world that remains is a world of men, and a world of homoerotic if not homosexual desire. Bloom wishes to recover a world in which very ugly men—men who stutter and drip gravy on their shirts—become objects of desire. The young man hopes "to meet his Socrates in the Agora"; the desiring eye looks on the decaying body and sees an aristocrat veiled in flesh. The old exclusive institutions open, but just wide enough for Bloom, and perhaps for you, to enter. When you enter, the whole world of exclusive enjoyments, of once-closed clubs and special privileges, of undeserved rewards opens before you. You enter a world which once was and is no longer, but perhaps—just perhaps—might live again.

Harvard, Yale, and Princeton are, Bloom tells us, not what they used to be. "There is hardly a Harvard man or a Yale man anymore." Once these universities were citadels of a republican (if not a democratic) aristocracy. They produced gentlemen as well as scholars. Men in boaters and blazers, with distinctive drawls, serried ranks of ancestors behind them and fat bank accounts before them, could visit wounding little slights on "the unclubbable." Now these universities are open to anyone with a good academic record, even women, Bloom wrote, and especially blacks. Universities have abandoned the "exclusion of outsiders, especially Jews." Bloom could enter the world of the Ivy League (Cornell and Chicago, if not Harvard and Yale), but he could not enter the world of the aristocracy, he could not become what he regarded as a gentleman, he could not enjoy the pleasures of exclusion.

Bloom was afflicted with the disease that Nietzsche diagnosed so acutely, *ressentiment*. Those who read Bloom with the most pleasure, with the most unaffected longing and the strongest passions, are those who have come recently, and perhaps not altogether securely, to privilege. The Dinesh D'Souzas and the Bill Kristols, the Francis Fukuyamas and the Eugene Genoveses affirmed hierarchies and exclusions as the round-shouldered, soft-handed boys of my youth boasted of masculine superiority. They were testing the waters. They claimed a right to exclude that those they aligned themselves with would never have granted them. If the excluded took offence, the claimed privilege was confirmed, and they could enjoy, for however brief a moment, the pleasures of hierarchy. Their pleasure was, however, dependent on the liberality of liberals and the good manners of all. A liberal could be relied on not to ask, "But aren't you gay?" Those with good manners would never ask, "Is it true that your father was a plumber?" or "Do you consider yourself white?" The liberal and the principled had fought for the inclusion of Jews. The recognition that the pleasures of hierarchy could be guaranteed only by the generosity of others sharpens the *ressentiment*. Status becomes a stolen pleasure.

Bloom and his cohort are like children who steal into an exclusive swimming club and feel both pride in their cleverness and a secret shame. They have gotten in, and no one has noticed that they don't belong. The knowing, the *arrivistes*, the connoisseurs of class, have fooled everyone. What some won by their breeding or their money, they have won by their wits. They can congratulate themselves on their cleverness, but as they do they fear that they will be found out and publicly shamed. They can feel contempt for the ordinary people who remain outside, but they know that now those people will look down on them as dishonest. They can feel contempt for the lazy, nonchalant people inside who don't notice that they don't belong, but as they do, they feel a sharper fear. They may already have been found out. There might be someone who nodded to the guard and said, "Those boys are my guests." Class in the closet is a masochist's pleasure.

That is the world of Bloom's desires. The world of Bloom's fears is a curious place as well. That world seems a paradise to me. In that world, where there are no longer Harvard men or Yale men, students win admission "not because of anything other than natural talent and hard work at their studies." College is open to rich and poor, "for the country is largely middle class now, and scholarship aid is easily available for those who are unable to pay." Students whose parents had not finished college came: "With the G.I. Bill, college was for everyone." People whose parents had lived in small ethnic enclaves went out into the world. A student whose father had "struggled to shake off" the "social disadvantages" of being an Italian or a Jew, Chinese or Japanese, came to college unburdened. He could make friends with whom he chose, he could marry whom he chose, he could choose to recover the customs of his ancestors or leave them behind. No door that mattered would be closed to him.

That world has never been. I am the first of my family to get a graduate degree. My parents were the first of their families to go to college, my father to the Naval Academy. They married outside their religions. We all made friends with whom we chose. America has opened the world to us. But I have also stood with friends as they married outside their religions, in weddings neither family would attend. I have seen Jews faced with dishes of shrimp and bacon at Princeton faculty dinners. Friends of mine who have the misfortune of being too tall, too strong, and too black have too often been stopped by the campus police. Race matters, as Cornel West wrote, and not simply as a matter of intellectual inquiry. We have not yet reached the world Bloom found so profoundly unsatisfactory. We are farther from it now than we have been in many years.

Much has changed in the years since Bloom published *The Closing of the American Mind*. I taught in the Ivy League then, as I do now. We saw our classes change in the 1980s. When I began to teach we had many middle-class students. Most of my students now are wealthy. They went to private schools and took special classes for the SATs. They can afford to take unpaid internships in the summer. Often they have family friends in the House or the Senate or at the World Bank who can find a place for them. They have nearly always been to Europe. There are still a few students whose families are poor: sent to school on full scholarship. Those I see have gone to private schools on scholarship. They have lived for a long time in a world divided between privilege and deprivation. If the students are middle class—I see fewer and fewer of them—they and their parents are burdened by debt. More often, they have gone elsewhere. The wealthy—those who went to private schools, who can afford to take unpaid internships, who vacation in Europe—often think of themselves as middle class. Their easy assumption that any middle-class person can afford what they can afford makes life hard for those who have to work to pay for college, who have to ask how much the books cost for each course they take, who have to wonder how they will repay their loans. My students are more ethnically diverse than those Bloom saw at Cornell, but they are less diverse by class. Other hierarchies remain as well. Bloom reinforced them.

Two phrases, repeated, serve as the echoing refrain to Bloom's discussion of the universities: "especially Jews" and "especially blacks." These phrases enable us to orient ourselves in the world Bloom lays out. In that world, where hierarchies are to remain or be revived, they tell us who is up and who is down, who is, in Bloom's terms, "clubbable" or "unclubbable." If proper standards—in status, in morals, in aesthetics—are to be restored, then we must know the high and the low, the good and the bad, the beautiful and the ugly. We must learn to see, as Bloom sees, the beauty of the decayed aristocrat, the virtues of hierarchy. We must know who deserves to rise, and who deserves to be put down. Bloom tells us that—once—outsiders were excluded, "especially Jews." Now, he writes, formerly excluded groups have been brought into the university, "especially blacks." Once, he reminds us, qualified Jews were barred from the universities. Now he claims, the universities admit blacks who are "manifestly unqualified and unprepared."

Bloom takes the language of anti-Semitism, the old slurs, the old resentments, and turns it from Jews to blacks. It was wrong to say and do these things to Jews, Bloom recognizes, but he is all too ready to say and do those things to blacks. Blacks, Bloom insists, are different—and, Bloom argues, like the most hackneyed of anti-Semites, they bring it on themselves. Jews were excluded by others. Blacks, Bloom tells us, segregate themselves. Jews were excluded against their will. Blacks, Bloom tells us, mark themselves out, they refuse inclusion. "'They stick together' was a phrase often used in the past about this or that distinctive group, but it has become true, by and large, of the black students." Exclusivity made Jews victims, it makes blacks privileged. The old slurs, once directed at Jews, were lies, but Bloom claims they have "become true" of blacks. They are an exclusive group, they refuse to associate with others, they keep to their own kind. The state gives them special privileges. They profit from it. They are a problem. They have "proved indigestible."

Soon after *The Closing of the American Mind* was published, a woman I had just met asked me what I thought of it. I told her and she giggled. "I love it," she said. "It supports all my prejudices." She worked for the University of Chicago Business School in a position that, not so very many years before, would have been closed to women. Doors had opened for her. She wanted to close them behind her. She knew, and was willing to admit, with a little embarrassment, a little shame, what Bloom had given her.

The Closing of the American Mind sought exactly that. The doors that had opened in Bloom's time—to Americans from every European backwater, Jew and Catholic—were opening a little wider: to African Americans and South Asians, Muslims and Hindus. Bloom sought to close them. The minds that had opened a little wider were to be closed as well. The universities that had opened to the refugee scholars of Europe—to Strauss and Arendt, Freud and Einstein—had opened minds to new forms of thought, to psychoanalysis and the theory of relativity, to new theories of politics and new ways of reading. They were opening more every day, and with that came calls for other forms of opening: for integration, and free speech, for the recognition that African faces are beautiful and African novels literature. These were the minds Bloom sought to close.

5   *Getting the Natural Right*

Natural Right and History is said to argue for a return to truth, to a standard common to all and grounded in nature. Perhaps that reading is correct. If so, *Natural Right and History* presents nature as the realm of self-evident truths. In most of his writings, Strauss is careful to present nature not as the realm of certainty, of "pure and whole knowledge," but as the unexplored, uncharted territory of a "pure and whole questioning." Nature was not the site of certainty, nature was the realm of the unknown, the inchoate, of that which might be known but wasn't, of that which might be known but was not yet. Nature was a riddle: a place of possibilities, a place of questions. Nature was a beginning, a resource, out of which people and worlds could be fashioned. The mysterious and enduring first nature of man remains a question Strauss explored to the end of his life.

How much turns on this understanding of nature? Science, politics, and virtue are all at stake here. Natural scientists, catching sight of the double helix structure of DNA, learning the complex code of the genome, seeing from far away the traces of water on Mars, of light at the edge of the universe, hearing the speech of dolphins, reading the texts of limestone, learn, as they learn more, how little we know, how many questions are before us. Nature spreads out a vast unexplored terrain, full of dangers, yes, but also full of pleasures and discoveries. These scientists see the invitation of the unknown in nature, they know the pleasures of the question, and they still explore. Political scientists and philosophers, sociologists and anthropologists, who look at the natural in the human and see the same vast unexplored terrain, will do the same. They will know, in the time-honored precept of Socrates, that they do not know. They will question, they will explore. They will learn, and take pleasure in learning.

The political Straussians are less concerned with natural rights than with getting the natural right. Nature, in their view, has but one form. That form is simple and certain, stable and secure. Nature, in these accounts, is the realm of certain and self-evident truths. Strauss's "pure and whole questioning" is abandoned by these Straussians for safer if more suspect certainties. We can be sure, so they tell us, about what is natural and unnatural. Common sense tells us all we need to know. They forget that common sense—as Socrates, Rousseau, and other philosophers should have reminded them—belongs not to nature but to our second natures. Common sense is the sense of the community.

Nature speaks to the Straussians in the dulcet accents of mid-twentieth-century popular culture. Nature says that marriage (and what could nature know of marriage?) is between a man and a women, and sex is for procreation. Nature says that it is natural for men to have authority over women, and the final word on finances. Nature says that women are emotional and men philosophic. Nature, in these accounts, sounds strangely like the Next to the Last Man, not quite secure, threatened by dangers all around him, resenting the burdens of a demanding life.

In *The Hungry Soul*, Leon Kass, chairman of the Presidential Council on Bioethics, writes of this domesticated nature. This is an elegant and charming book. In it learning becomes playful and inviting. Nietzsche wrote that his work might be initially a little tough to chew on, a little difficult to digest, but "it will grow on you, I swear." *The Hungry Soul* goes down easy, except perhaps, when one gets to ice cream. Kass has an admiring public at Chicago and on the Web, but his strictures on the eating of ice cream have been hard for some to swallow. Licking an ice cream cone, Kass writes, is a "catlike activity that has been made acceptable in informal America but that still offends those who know eating in public is offensive. . . . I fear I may by this remark lose the sympathy of many readers, people who will condescendingly regard as quaint or even priggish the view that eating in the street is for dogs." Catlike or doglike, it is, in Kass's view, "shameful behavior." The one who walks and eats, Kass writes, is simply led by appetite.

Whether we exercise self-control or not, we are all led by appetite. Eating—the need for food, the fierce demands of appetite, the inexorable consequences of eating too much or too little—is a constant reminder that our first nature is alive in us. An old story held that Alexander the Great hated to eat because eating reminded him of his mortality. Eating reminds us all of our likeness not only to one another but to animals who—like us—must eat. Eating reminds us that we are vulnerable, bound by the demands of our own nature, and the vagaries of nature outside us. Cooking and table manners, the duties of host and guest, go to the heart of civilization because they speak to the need for food common to us all.

The hungry soul shows civilization as the realm of the soul, of thought and reflection. The hungry body might draw our attention to other aspects of civilization. The need for food reminds us that we are embedded in the natural world: vulnerable to the effects of flood and drought, locusts and hail. There are other threats to the food supply as well. Politics and the market bring new hazards to the food supply. The practices of civilized agriculture—from terracing and irrigation to antibiotics and genetic modification—bring new dangers with them. One might ask whether our souls are well fed when our bodies dine on beef fed sheep brains. None of this appears in *The Hungry Soul*. Man's relations with nature are presented as requiring only thought and changes in one's own household to set them right.

Kass undertakes, with equal charm, to tell Americans not only how they ought to eat but how they ought to think of romance, marry, and produce children, how happiness should be earned, and how they should mourn. In *Wing to Wing, Oar to Oar,* he and his wife reflect on their own courtship and marriage. In *Beyond Therapy: Biotechnology and the Pursuit of Happiness,* Kass and the members of the President's Council on Bioethics provide guidance on what it means to be happy. Collaboration with his wife and the other members of the President's Council might seem to account for the pervasive use of "we" in these works, but the explanation doesn't hold: Kass uses "we" just as often in books he writes alone. The assumption that he speaks for "us," that we are all enfolded in the warm glow of agreement, doesn't sit well with all readers. "Well, *I* am just a mere *me!*" a blogger at *Classical Values* quite correctly declares. "I am no more of a 'we' than Kass is." But Kass does speak for us, and with the prestige, if not the power, of the state behind him.

Happiness, the ancients said, is the end of man, but neither we nor the ancients have been sure of how happiness is to be achieved. The discussion in *Beyond Therapy* acknowledges that Americans secured freedom for the pursuit of happiness and that the ancients (like the moderns) differed on what happiness might be. The Council on Bioethics is not so modest. Happiness is "inseparable from the pleasure that comes from the perfecting of our natures and living fruitfully with our families, friends and fellow citizens." This would seem to lead simply to another set of questions. What are our natures? How are we to live fruitfully? Is living a fruitful life as a Mormon mother the same as living a fruitful life as an army colonel? Are fruitful lives always in accord with one another? Is living well with our families, friends, and fellow citizens always a pleasure? Can duty produce unhappiness? Can honorable lives come into conflict? The council directs the questioning away from a broader inquiry and into easier, less troubling channels. We emerge, having read a little Shakespeare, having asked a few questions, with opinions intact.

The books published by the council, seem, like the works of the council's chairman, Leon Kass, to be works of reflection in the intellectual sense: of thought, and long consideration. Yet they seem to me to be too close to reflection in another sense, the sense of vanity. These works hold up a mirror into which the author and the like-minded reader look with pleasure. They can admire the shape of their lives. They can see in their actions, in their choices, what is good for human beings, and what must therefore be natural to them. They believe that what they see in that mirror, in their reflections, is natural and true.

Mirrors distort. The image of nature the mirror shows is not nature but convention. Too often, those conventions are not examined but admired.

The admiration comes as one form of reflection, masquerades as another. The council's books appear to be works of reflection-

as-thought. There are references to works of literature, quotations from Shakespeare (many) and other poets (a few), references to the natural sciences and to popular culture. Questions
are asked, alternatives are weighed, consequences considered.
But are they? Read carefully. Read as if you too were part of this
debate, and you will find that questions go unasked, alternatives go unexamined, and objections are silenced. Convention,
what "we" do, is reaffirmed. Reflection-as-thought gives way to
reflection-as-vanity. Questions are answered not by reason but
by reference to what Kass has called "the wisdom of repugnance." The wisdom of repugnance is, in plain English, the belief that what disgusts us must be bad.

I'd like to bring in another authority here, an eminent doctor,
highly regarded in American letters: Dr. Seuss. In his famous
work *Green Eggs and Ham* the magisterial doctor makes a frontal
assault on the wisdom of repugnance. Sam-I-Am offers a creature a taste of the titular dish. The resistant creature refuses, repeatedly and emphatically, moved by that wisdom of repugnance. "I do not like green eggs and ham, I do not like them
Sam-I-Am," the creature repeatedly pronounces. Sam persists,
and the creature, finally persuaded to taste the repugnant green
eggs and ham, exclaims, "I do like green eggs and ham." Another
eminent doctor, Dr. Johnson, observed that it "was a brave man
that first et an oyster" and thought that heroic epicure to be commended. If we were to follow the wisdom of repugnance in eating, the greatest wisdom would undoubtedly be found in Ludwig

Wittgenstein, who lived for a year on cottage cheese and rye bread; my old friend Bart Schultz, who ate cheese pizza and salad; or nearly any two-year-old.

Repugnance, the good doctors suggest, is not a reliable guide to cuisine. It is not a good guide to ethics, either. Some of us are, to our regret, old enough to remember that once some white people thought it repugnant to share a water fountain or a bathroom or a seat on the bus with a black person. The wisdom of repugnance has filled the repertoire of justifications for racial and religious persecution: they are ugly, they are violent, they have nasty habits (cooking with garlic!) and too many children. Some of the practices presently justified by appeals to the wisdom of repugnance might make the council think again about its merits. Would they find it, for example, an adequate justification for clitoridectomy?

Marriage and manliness are two of the natural things dearest to the most political Straussians, two of the things most often given as natural, yet two congeries of practice most governed by convention. For the Straussians marriage is a natural institution. The natural end of marriage is the birth and education of children. If it accords to that end, they argue, marriage is natural. Understood in this way, marriage seems to accord very clearly to the conceptions held by the American right and the political issues of the early twenty-first century. Divorce, though perhaps distasteful, is not unnatural. Gay marriages, however responsible, faithful, or loving, are unnatural. Polygamous marriages, and childless marriages willfully held to, are not matters of intense public debate (in this place, at this time) and need not trouble reflection very far.

Children come into the world not through marriage, but through sex. Sex—and the preservation of the species—can take place outside marriage. In fact, children can be produced and the species preserved outside the joining of a man and a woman in sex. All that requires is the fertilization of an egg by a sperm, and the development of the fertilized egg into a viable child. The first need not be done in a human body, the second need not be done in the womb of the woman who gave the egg. Mothers can become mothers through adoption, or even through action over a long stretch of time, as a woman (often a sister or an aunt, or another of the father's wives) takes on the care of a child.

Yet even if we set these things aside, we are far from seeing marriage as a natural institution. If we do, we lose sight of much that is important in marriage, and much of its virtue and honor and romance as well. Marriage joins families as well as individuals, and it joins individuals not merely to each other, or to each other's families, but to the community. Marriage is a matter of law and contract, conferring legal obligations. Marriage binds people not only to each other, but to their duties. Marriage is thus a discipline that people are taught, formally and informally, by parents, teachers, priests, rabbis, and advice columnists. Marriage is what happens at the end of the fairy tale or the romance novel, when the hero and heroine live "happily ever after." Marriage is an end (and a beginning) that children (especially girls) are taught to imagine as triumphant happiness. Marriage is a matter of contract, custom and convention, myth and romance, fairy tales and legal structures. Very little in it is natural at all.

Hadley Arkes, one of marriage's most vociferous defenders among the Straussians, insists, "Marriage cannot be detached from what some might call the 'natural teleology of the body': namely, the inescapable fact that only two people, not three, only a man and a woman, can beget a child." He is quite right. Marriage cannot be detached from "the natural teleology of the body" because it is designed in response to it. Marriage is not natural. Marriage manages nature. Marriage, Hadley Arkes insists, is connected to "the inescapable fact" that sex between two people, "a man and a woman, can beget a child." And though this is true of only certain kinds of sex and only some of the time, it is inescapably true that children are often a consequence, and (though Arkes is too squeamish to say this) a consequence that, in nature, is all too easy to ignore. Marriage brings the force of law, custom, morality, and imagination to the protection of children.

That, however, radically underestimates the uses of marriage. Like most institutions that appear in different forms and places, and endure over a long span of time, marriage is good for quite a few things. Marriage provides care to otherwise motherless, fatherless children; and "for richer, for poorer, in sickness and in health," to the poor and the ill as well. In these relations, over time, people learn new forms of love. Marriage unites people, enabling them to make lives spanning generations. Marriage helps direct sexuality: less by controlling what people do than by channeling (especially in young girls) what they wish to do. Marriage helps order the property, especially after death. Civilizations have found marriage a good tool for managing the natural (and, as it happens, elements of the moral, the economic, and the political). As time has passed, it has been put to more uses. We should not be surprised at suggestions that it be used to manage other forms of sexuality. We should be amused at the ironies.

There are sadder and more troubling ironies in the council's considerations of happiness. Happiness, we are told, is something one should deserve. Few, I think, have the confidence to assume that their happiness is wholly deserved. Most of us think that happiness is not wholly our work. Many of those things that make for happiness: loving and being loved, having talents and being able to use them, seeing and hearing (touching and smelling) the beautiful, seem to owe as much to grace and good luck as to any work of ours.

Those whose well-being, if not their happiness, is secured by selective serotonin reuptake inhibitors (SSRIs) like Prozac or Zoloft will not be reassured by the council's considerations. They may be enjoying an undeserved happiness, or perhaps merely an undeserved respite from deserved unhappiness. Those who love them will be disturbed as well. The council asks, If someone who loves you takes Prozac, does she, does he, *really* love you? If you take Prozac and love someone, how do you know he or she loves *you?* Aren't these loved ones merely loving the drug? These questions are disturbing. They are not, however, enlightening. They are manipulative.

They are also far less compelling than they at first appear. The council does not ask these questions of those who take, for example, thyroid medication, yet these people would be quite different if they did not take their medicine. Consider the woman taking Prozac. Kass has her husband ask, "Just *to whom* am I married? Would I love Sally if she stopped taking Prozac?" The same questions could be asked of a woman taking thyroid medication. Without it, she would rapidly succumb to Hashimoto's disease. She would grow yellow, fat, and unattractive. Worse, her mind and her personality would alter. Would Kass—would we—have the husband ask, "Just *to whom* am I married? Would I love Sally if she stopped taking Synthroid?"

If one follows the council's questions (and implicit answers) like a trail of breadcrumbs through the woods, one will arrive where the council does: full of the council's suspicions, and convinced that these things are against nature. If the reader asks the questions the author has set aside, the path will disappear in a forest of speculation. The reader will have returned to "pure and whole questioning."

By letting vanity masquerade as reflection, and dressing convention in the garb of nature, by silencing experiment and inquiry with the "wisdom of repugnance," the council, or the council's chairman, has given us reassuring illusions and the comfort of convention. Nature provides a refuge from questioning, science a weapon of defense against assaults on convention.

Strauss's conception of nature as best approached by "a pure and whole questioning" leads to a science of exploration, discovery, and investigation. The conception of nature as a realm of certainties makes nature a political resource. If nature is the realm of certainties, then nature can furnish certain principles for how people should live their lives. These principles, being natural, would apply to all human beings. They would not require acceptance. No one could question them. Nature, in this form, licenses an authoritarian politics: people can be made to obey what is in their own—certain—interest. Nature, in this form, authorizes totalitarianism. All of life—eating, dining, sex, marriage, children, happiness, mourning, and death—is natural. All of life, if properly understood, reveals the presence of these guiding principles.

Following this understanding of nature has eased the politicization of the sciences. If nature's God had revealed the truths of science to religion, scientific inquiry could—and should—be subject to direction. The President's Council on Bioethics is one of the means for directing the sciences, and it has been employed aggressively. When I began this book, in the fall of 2003, the President's Council on Bioethics was predominately Straussian.

That influence was evident not only among council members but also in the council staff. In February 2004 two of the remaining voices of dissent were removed from the council and replaced with three new appointees. Elizabeth Blackburn and William May "were often in the minority on the Council as they provided dissenting views," the Associated Press reported. Blackburn herself told the *Washington Post* that she was dismissed because her views did not accord with those of Leon Kass. She has said that when she joined the council, she initially found the discussions wide-ranging. "Yet at council meetings, I consistently sensed resistance to presenting human embryonic stem cell research in a way that would acknowledge the scientific, experimentally verified realities." She sought out the most advanced scientific information from her fellow cell biologists and placed this before the council. "The information I submitted was not reflected in the report drafts." Kass was, Blackburn told the *Washington Post*, "stacking the council with the compliant."

Leon Kass responded: "Even before the President's Council on Bioethics had its first meeting in January 2002, charges were flying that the council was stacked with political and religious conservatives. . . . The charges were malicious and false then, as they are now." No one, Kass writes, who read the transcripts of the council's meetings or the council's publications, could doubt its diversity. Blackburn attended those meetings, found them less than open, and had her opposition censored. I have read transcripts of the hearings and the council's publications. Though I do not know Dr. Blackburn, I join her in doubting the council's diversity. The council was not merely "stacked with political and religious conservatives"; it showed a single dominant influence. The nominees of February 2004 only enhanced that influence.

Blackburn was former president of the Society of Cell Biology. William May was a medical ethicist and retired professor from Southern Methodist University. They were replaced by Diana Schaub, Peter Lawler, and Benjamin Carson, a pediatric neuro-surgeon. Carson's appointment has been, because of his medical credentials, the least controversial, though his avowed conservatism further narrows the already narrow council. Schaub is a political theorist from Loyola College in Maryland who works on Montesquieu. Lawler, a political theorist from Berry College in Georgia, is the author of a book called *Aliens in America: The Strange Truth About Our Souls*. A link from Lawler's website offers quotations from his classes. To take the first three of a "Top 50," "Machiavelli is a Sinatra kind of guy," "College Football keeps people from revolting," and "Use your money for pink Cadillacs, pink flamingos and all sorts of other pink things." The quotations were provided by his students. Students are fond of recording the frivolous and the amusing, and the top three quotations, though they seem silly, ought not to trouble us too much. But we might doubt the propriety of an appointee who would tell his class, "Democrats think theory is a waste of time."

Kass writes of Lawler and Schaub, "Both are known among their colleagues for their openness to discourse and their devotion to public deliberation and democratic decision-making. Their personal views on the matters to come before the council in the coming term are completely unknown." Setting aside Professor Lawler's views on Democrats, I would not question the first claim. On the contrary, I have met Professor Schaub, and I have always found her "open to discourse." The second claim is disingenuous at best. Lawler and Schaub are both Straussians, both had published on related questions, and both had expressed views close to those of Leon Kass before they were appointed to the council. They did so, in at least one case, in front of him. Kass, Lawler, and Schaub all participated in a discussion of *Beyond Therapy* at the American Enterprise Institute on December 9, 2003.

When asked about these changes in the composition of the committee, a spokesman for President Bush said, "We decided to appoint other people with other expertise and experience." In one sense, they—or rather, President Bush—did exactly that. A distinguished medical ethicist and the former president of the Society of Cell Biology were replaced by two political theorists from minor academic institutions. Yet because the political theorists come from the same school of thought, one might more accurately say that they added not "different expertise" but, however thoughtful they might be, more of the same.

The influence of the Straussians and their allies on science extends beyond the influence of Kass and his Council on Bioethics. In the winter of 2003–4 a team of scientists, including twenty

Nobel laureates, issued a statement asserting, as the *New York Times* reported, that "the Bush administration had systematically distorted scientific fact in the service of policy goals on the environment, health, biomedical research and nuclear weaponry at home and abroad." The report followed a minority congressional investigation, commissioned by Representative Henry Waxman, a Democrat from California, into the politicization of science. The conclusions of both investigations were supported by scientists who had served in both Republican and Democratic administrations and have troubled scientists of all political persuasions.

As the report on the natural and physical sciences was issued, major organizations in the social sciences and the humanities prepared to respond to congressional attempts to exercise control over research in area studies. The Higher Education Act Reauthorization Bill (HR 3077) sought the reauthorization of funds for what is popularly called Title VI. Title VI funds provide support for the study of foreign languages and for area studies centers, including those studying the Middle East, India and Pakistan, China, and East Asia. The initial rationale for the funding had been, in part, that Americans knew too little of areas of the world that might pose threats to our security in the future. Title VI has funded, for example, language study in Arabic and Farsi, the language spoken in Iran. After 9/11, the need for competent speakers of Arabic, and for scholars with profound knowledge of the Arab and Islamic worlds, seemed all the more evident.

HR 3077 sought, however, not to encourage area studies and language studies but to constrain them. Area studies centers would be placed under an oversight committee whose members would be appointed by the government. The oversight committee was to ensure that the area studies centers represented an appropriate range of political perspectives—to be determined by the politically appointed committee members—and that the centers met the "information and manpower needs of American business." Education was to be subordinated to the interests of private corporations; funding for research (and even teaching positions) was to be under government surveillance. Many academic organizations, including the American Association of University Professors and the American Political Science Association, wrote letters protesting the oversight provisions in HR 3077, but even the presidents of these associations found it impossible to get a hearing before the congressional committees concerned.

We in the American academy have grown accustomed to freedom of research, to pursuing knowledge for its own sake. The idea of having to satisfy the ideological requirements of a government agent is foreign to us. There had been a period in the 1980s when scholars feared that the National Endowment for the Humanities was making its decisions in part on the basis of an ideological litmus test. Those days seemed to have passed. Now, twenty years later, the government is countenancing far more intrusive attempts to govern the academy and hold professors to an ideological orthodoxy.

The year before HR 3077, President Bush had appointed Daniel Pipes to the board of the United States Institute for Peace. The appointment was controversial, not least because Pipes had participated in the formation of Campus Watch. Campus Watch recruited students for projects reminiscent of the Straussian truth squads, but with a higher degree of organization. They were to vigorously represent in classes the views of Pipes's organization on Middle Eastern politics and history. They were to tell professors what books they should have on their reading lists—and which books they should remove. Young men and women with lists printed from the Campus Watch website showed up after class to interrogate their professors. Why were books condemned by Campus Watch on the reading list? The Campus Watch people were not averse to advertising their own books, and an element of profit making entered under the guise of ideological purity. Professors who did not comply by putting Daniel Pipes or Martin Kramer on the reading list were to be reported. Anonymous reports were posted on the Campus Watch website, unverified. Campus Watch posted an enemies list. Harassment followed.

These techniques did not sit well with professors, even with some who shared the political preferences of Campus Watch. They wrote in, first proudly asking for the honor of inclusion on the enemies list, then with a little more irreverence, nominating each other. Dan Brumberg of Georgetown University and Steve Heydemann, then of Columbia, wrote masterpieces of the genre, nominating each other. "Dear Marty [Kramer] and Daniel [Pipes]," Heydemann wrote, "This effort is long overdue. For too many years we have sat idly by while ideologues of the most despicable kind have wormed their way into our universities, nibbling, nibbling at the core of American higher education until it has become nothing but the pits. I am referring, of course, to 'scholars' such as Daniel Brumberg, whom I believe you may know (a fact which, whether true or not, you would be well advised to explain)." Brumberg, Heydemann goes on to report with mock horror, has made his next project "a thinly veiled attempt to dupe Americans into viewing Islam as a 'religion.' . . . Clearly, something must be done about Brumberg." These postings were in the best tradition of a free and fearless academy. They were not entirely successful. The enemies list is gone, but Campus Watch thrives. All over the United States, as they prepare their classes and make up their reading lists, professors ask themselves not only, "What are the best books for my students?" but "Can I afford to offend Campus Watch?" As they teach their classes they wonder, "Who in this class might inform on me?"

6   *Persecution and the Art of Writing*

All Straussians are bound together by a certain regard for the text, by practices of reading, by a net of allusions and references, by stories and practices. The net binds others with them: Talmudic scholars and poststructuralists, theorists of many kinds. Some groups among the Straussians may be bound by other secrets, whether these are really secrets or not. Like the supposedly secret manuscript that Cropsey took from his file cabinet to hand to me, some of these supposed secrets may be in extensive circulation.

No one, for example, should be surprised to learn that the students of Strauss hold Nietzsche and Heidegger in high regard. These philosophers have been taught in open classes, and with great respect, for many years. Though it is supposed to be a dangerous thing to say in modern (or postmodern) America, no one will be surprised to learn that Straussians believe all men are not created equal in their intellectual capacities. Nor will anyone be shocked to learn that some people are thought to be more able than others to read philosophy, and that only a few are able to write it. Finally, I do not think I will destroy the social order—or even let the cat out of the bag—if I tell you that Straussians think that certain ideas are dangerous except to the well educated and the wise.

There is no secret that is wholly secret. The secret is, paradoxically, not something altogether hidden but something at least partly known. If you have a secret, it is something you know. If you tell me a secret, then it is something known between us. The secret is at once a hidden thing and a revealed one: something revealed to us, something hidden from others. Secrets entail a bond. The students of Bloom were bound together by what they refused to acknowledge in public, by what they would not say there but said readily in private and among themselves. The secret was a bond not because it was held silently but because it was revealed privately and only to a few. The hidden word binds a set of people to one another. This is, I suspect, what animates both secrets and the rumors of secrets among the Straussians.

Secret teachings take several forms. In any text of any difficulty there are levels of accessibility. There are things you may understand now and other things that will become apparent when you have read the text and considered it as a whole. There are still other things that will become apparent to you over time, as you grow more learned, more thoughtful, or more experienced. There are some things, in all likelihood, that will never be apparent to you, but remain for someone else to see. Some call these levels of difficulty "secret teachings" and act as if they are given only to initiates. There is nothing secret about them at all. They are there in the open for anyone—who can—to read.

There is another form of secret teaching. This concerns politics, and it is taken up in Strauss's book *Persecution and the Art of Writing*. In some places (in most places), in some times (in most times), there are things that cannot be said without danger. One could not say, in the Athens of Socrates, that "the sun is a stone and the moon earth," or that one did not "believe in the gods the city believes in." These are the accusations brought against Socrates in the *Apology*, the charges that bring about his death. In every regime, in every time, in every place, there are things that cannot be said without provoking anger, outrage, and danger. If one persists in thinking these things and wishes to tell them to others, one needs to do so with subtlety or take the risk. If the police knock at the door, if the government prosecutor picks up the book, one might wish to say, "This text does not violate the law." Workers do this when they criticize the boss. Diplomats do it when they deliver a little warning. Politicians do it when they want to speak to one set of interests without alienating another. Philosophers do it when they fear the state, the church, or the anger of the people.

The art of writing under persecution thus consists for the most part of hiding in plain sight. Concealment is effective only if it overcomes itself. The purpose of concealment is to ensure not that some ideas are hidden and remain so, but rather that these ideas are preserved when they might be lost, transmitted when they might be quarantined, circulated when they might be contained. The esoteric, the hidden, the concealed must become open, must circulate, if the strategy is to be successful. The strategy aims not at concealment but at preservation, transmission, and openness: so that ideas which might otherwise be lost can continue.

This desire to preserve, to uncover, may account in part for the popularity of digging as metaphor in political theory. Lacan once remarked that he had given his listeners "the machinery to dig this field. . . . I have given them the plough and the ploughshare." His metaphor suggests that he, like most philosophers, hoped something would come to light in that field. In *Persecution and the Art of Writing*, Strauss gave his readers new tools to dig with. The aim of these tools, these techniques, these rediscovered ways of reading, was not to conceal but to reveal. Strauss's students learned to read what the author had hidden in plain sight.

The Straussians have had other uses for these tools. Strauss revealed, they have concealed. They have forwarded another understanding of secret teachings. In this view some ideas must be permanently concealed from the uninitiated. These ideas are too dangerous for the masses (that is to say, for ordinary people). They may lead to rebellion, or impiety, to the reading of Nietzsche or the recognition of civil unions. If possible these dangerous and tempting ideas should be concealed from the uninitiated elite as well, lest these irresponsible ones circulate dangerous truths to the unwashed. In this fashion, Puritan divines once objected to the listing of sins, so that the innocent might not be tempted, and priests taught their parishioners not to read the Bible alone, lest they be led into error.

Strauss taught his students (as any good interpreter would) to look for gaps in the text; to see what is not said and ask "why?" We can use these tools to read the Straussians. Attention to silences requires that one distinguish that which is not cited from that which is not read. When Bloom writes that deconstruction destroys meaning, or another Straussian characterizes Lacan as a Marxist, it's clear that Derrida and Lacan haven't been read. The charge of "nihilism" is flung about so freely that it rarely means more than "I don't like that" or "I wish those people did not exist." These silences indicate a lack of reading, a lack of knowledge.

That lack of knowledge is not merely accidental. It is enforced. I left Chicago after graduate school and went for a year to the Pembroke Center at Brown University. While I was there, I met a literary theorist named Kaja Silverman who suggested that I read Lacan, the French psychoanalytic theorist and philosopher. Lacan is an intense pleasure to anyone trained as I was. His writing is elegantly structured. Find the folds and hinges, and it opens before you like a piece of origami or a child's Transformer. If you have read Plato, Lacan has witticisms and insights for you;

if you have read Hegel, you will have still more. I had been taught to read for this. My teachers, however, took another view. They never told me directly not to read this (or Foucault or Derrida, my other reading of that moment), but they sent messages through my friends that they were "very disturbed" and "very unhappy." Not having felt the pull of the leash before, I thought this absurd. We were scholars and read without fear or favor, or so I thought, and I scoffed at their misgivings. After the third or fourth time, I asked a friend what my professors had gotten their knickers in a twist about. She smiled at me and said, "You have gone over to the dark side of the Force."

There are other, deeper and more deliberate silences. Consider a book by Thomas Pangle, an eminent student of Strauss and professor at the University of Toronto, *Political Philosophy and the God of Abraham*. The book has a curious silence. Though many commentaries on the sacrifice of Isaac are discussed in that work, there is no mention of the famous commentary by Jacques Derrida. Is this an error of ignorance? Pangle is a learned man. *The Gift of Death* is a well-known work. Pangle is an intelligent man, trained in the reading of texts; he cannot have failed to recognize the beauty and power of Derrida's reading. Pangle's argument responds not simply to Kierkegaard (whom he does cite) but to Derrida's reading of Kierkegaard. There is, however, no citation of any of Derrida's writings on Abraham. There is one citation to Derrida. This citation tells me more clearly than a billboard by the highway that Pangle has read Derrida and wants some readers to know it. The citation is to an article entitled "How to Avoid Speaking."

This is a classic in the Straussian genre. Many allusions, like this, are amusing, and seem at first glance like nothing more than an author's little joke. Yet they use the seemingly frivolous, silly little allusion to mark a very serious, even a grave, reflection. That is the case here. A reference like this suggests *ressentiment*, or an inappropriate (but hardly unknown) form of "school spirit" in which the cognoscenti titter behind their hands at this witty bit of esoterica. The silencing of Derrida is due to something more. Perhaps it is piety.

Abraham, Kierkegaard writes, sacrifices Isaac: he abandons ethics for faith, abandons the good to follow the command of God. We see Abraham with fear and trembling. Derrida softens Kierkegaard's understanding of God, who holds back the knife, making Isaac the covenant that need not be fulfilled. Isaac, whose name means laughter, becomes the laughter of those who have been spared the necessity of fulfilling their covenant with God, the embodiment of divine mercy. Derrida does not, however, soften the teaching that all faith demands sacrifice. "Day after day, on all the Mount Moriahs of the world, I raise the knife over what I love." Pangle confronts Kierkegaard (and, silently, Derrida) with unease. Kierkegaard's is a "deeply disquieting claim." Pangle finds Kierkegaard's terrifying account "indecisive," and the reader is permitted to set it aside. Derrida's reading places God's mercy in the breaking of the covenant. There is an old tradition, held strongly among the Puritans, that evidence of God's mercy should be treated carefully. The Puritans feared that weak and sinful people might take the deity's mercy as a license to sin, like Catholics who know that confession can absolve them. (Those of us raised in that church may find the prospect of God's mercy something other than an enticement to sin.) Derrida's reading also suggests, more disturbingly, that the fulfillment of one set of responsibilities may demand the sacrifice of others. If doing one duty requires us to neglect other duties, if cultivating one virtue requires the sacrifice of others, then an all-encompassing perfection is beyond us. Each of us will be dependent on others to repair the duties we neglected. Each of us may someday be faced with someone who cultivated a virtue we sacrificed. I think that is something most of us are all too ready to acknowledge. Perhaps the danger lies in what follows. If this is true, if we do, if we must, sacrifice some virtues in cultivating others, then we must acknowledge that there is more than one good and honorable life. Some call this "moral relativism," and it makes them angry. I call it a simple recognition of the limits of a human life, and I take some comfort in knowing that the duties I could not fulfill and the virtues I had to sacrifice will show themselves in others, where I can depend on and admire them.

These strategies may aim at protecting the vulnerable, or at keeping some in ignorance. In two important respects, they depart from the strategies described and praised by Strauss. *Persecution and the Art of Writing* described the ways in which people who loved learning and wished to preserve it for others evaded the control of those who would persecute them, and transmitted what they had learned to others. They wrote and taught carefully in times of danger, and their learning lived on. In this understanding, secret teachings and esoteric writing are intended to preserve learning, so that knowledge may be passed to many others. Those who wrote in this way did not intend to keep teachings *from* those who wished to learn, but to keep teachings *for* them. Nor were these strategies of concealment used by and for the good of those in power. Jews in the Inquisition, the freethinking in religious realms, the disenfranchised, the excluded, the persecuted, employed these strategies against the powerful, against their rulers, against those who would persecute them. The art of writing, as Strauss described it, was a weapon of the weak. The forms of esoteric teaching advocated by the Straussians work in exactly the opposite way: to prevent the circulation of ideas, to preserve the powerful against criticism, to serve the strong and keep the weak vulnerable. The old practice of speaking truth to power is turned upside down in this form of esoteric teaching.

Pangle's concealment is a serious one. There is a significant omission, impelled by a serious intention. The questions are grave. The techniques of concealment are employed deliberately here, and to some purpose. The frivolous witticism of citing the silent Derrida only in "How to Avoid Speaking" hides a serious intention. Other Straussians are often simply silly.

Anyone who has spent time among the Straussians knows

their passion for puns, for partial quotations and allusions made to carry an insult, or simply as a form of amusement. You will have seen them count chapters or the number of things in a list. They are given, especially the lesser ones, to a fascination with *gamatria*. *Gamatria* is a kabbalistic practice which assigns significance to numbers. The numbers may have reference to things in the natural world (one's two eyes or ten fingers), to convention (the twelve months in a year, the seven days in a week), to years, to verses in the Bible, to special numbers like 3 or 9, or to the number of letters in the name of God (13×13, or 139). When I first heard Straussians saying things like "there are three chapters and three parts, and three times three is nine," I felt rather as if I had heard them casting runes, or reading Tarot cards. I asked my teacher whether people took this seriously. All too seriously, it turned out. For half an hour or so he regaled me with stories of silly things people did with *gamatria*. He finished up by pulling out an article. Look at footnote 139, he told me. "One hundred and thirty nine!" I said. "Why so many footnotes in a single article?" "He always has at least that many," he told me "so that he can mention himself in footnote 139."

The relation of Straussians to the art of writing seems to be a pattern of reversals. Strauss revealed, they conceal; the seemingly silly once pointed the way to the serious, now the serious seems devoted to the merely silly.

American culture at large seems afflicted by the same pattern of reversals in the art of writing. The serious become silly, the silly become serious. The media that once constituted the Fourth Estate, that made politics visible, now work to conceal it. Few have failed to notice that newspapers and the television news have given over more and more of the time once given to politics to the entertaining and the innocuous. People who pick up the newspaper or watch the TV as I write this might see news on the war in Iraq or the results of the latest election polls in the United States. They would read, even in the "newspaper of record," more local than national or international news. A local fire or child welfare scandal would command more coverage than the latest elections in Germany or a riot in Tehran. They could find more on fashion, sports, and health than on national and international politics combined. A few minutes of politics on the evening news would be followed by a sentimental "human interest story" and by detailed coverage on such important matters as the weight at death of the originator of the Atkins diet.

Politics has not been excised from the newspaper—it is all too present—but it is now very carefully, and very thoroughly, concealed. The sentimental, the personal, the touching stories of pets or children, the provision of advice, recipes, and scores—these have surpassed political reporting. The front page of my local paper, the *Philadelphia Inquirer*, has stories on football recruiting, the Flower Show, fires, the personal tribulations of local families. Ostensibly political coverage is often preoccupied with the personal: Dean's wife, Berlusconi's plastic surgery, Gerhard Schröder's hair. Correspondents on the campaign trail look out for gaffes rather than elaboration of the candidate's positions on issues. Gaffes are simple and factual. Issues are complicated, and it is difficult (perhaps impossible) for a correspondent to convey the candidate's position and the context and importance of the issue without indicating those things which are the substance of politics: loyalties and values. Television news is similarly skewed. There is a little news of some political significance, more news of less significance—usually concerning a celebrity or two—and then an in-depth story on a matter of health or finance.

As the serious press descends to the silly, the silly press grows satirical. Grocery store tabloids have articles which might not rank as news but offer some of the critical bite of older traditions of critical journalism. Consider this story from the *Weekly World News:* "Seven Congressmen Are Zombies" the headline reads. "But they blend in so well," the story continues that "no one—in the House or Senate—knows who they are." As the tabloids move from scandal to satire, journalistic standards in the respectable press decline.

A telling instance of this development was observed by the economist and *New York Times* columnist Paul Krugman. Richard Perle co-wrote a *Wall Street Journal* editorial praising a deal with Boeing. Perle wrote as a member of the Defense Policy Board but failed to indicate to the readers of the *Journal* that Boeing had invested in Perle's venture capital fund, Trireme Partners. George Will consults with and frequently praises Straussians in his *Washington Post* and *Newsweek* columns advancing conservative causes. He and William F. Buckley of the *National Review* have given particular attention to ethical issues and the decline of standards in the West. As Krugman discovered, however, their concern for ethics and propriety did not extend to their own conduct. Both Will and Buckley wrote columns praising the Canadian media mogul Conrad Black without revealing that they were paid advisers to a company he owned.

This is old news to academics, though not, perhaps, to college students, parents, and the public. The rise of conservative student newspapers across the United States in the 1990s was not a spontaneous phenomenon. The papers were often started, funded, and supplied with articles by conservative groups. The newspapers rarely mentioned these subsidies, or acknowledged that articles were provided not by students or student groups but by conservative journals. These publications were not, in the ordinary sense, student newspapers at all. There was something fundamentally dishonest in this. The students who presented those articles as student work in a student newspaper were no better than the students who hand in term papers bought from the notorious Dr. Evil's House of Cheat. The foundations and journals who furnished the articles acted as the House of Cheat themselves. Yet these newspapers complained long and bitterly about declining standards and moral indifference. They were right to worry that declining private morality would have political consequences. Twenty years later the Bush administration filmed favorable coverage of administration health policy and offered these videos to local television stations. Viewers would see an actor in the guise of a reporter asking the questions and getting the answers the administration preferred, yet they would not be told the piece was anything other than simple journalism.

Perhaps the most extraordinary inversion comes in engagements with the mass media. The mass media (not least because they are the *mass* media) are regularly deprecated in Straussian circles. Like other intellectuals, Straussians tend to regard the mass media as catering—or, rather, pandering—to the lowest tastes, perhaps even lowering those tastes. The mass media therefore constitute one of the sites identified as hostile territory. Yet the media have served these Straussian conservatives very well. Columnists like George Will consult them, recommend their books, and promote their ideas in the daily newspaper. Newspapers and journals—the *New York Times*, the *Wall Street Journal*, *Vanity Fair*—interview them and write articles on their influence. They publish widely circulated journals—the *Weekly Standard*, for example—and write for others: the *National Review*, the *New Republic*. They publish in other journals, less well known, circulating in smaller communities of thought, but perhaps equally influential: *First Things*, the *Claremont Review*, and the *New Criterion*. They may disdain postmodernity, but they are virtuosos of the Internet. Straussians have shown themselves adept at using the media: small and large, local and international. If the art of writing provides protection against persecution, the art of publishing provides a chance to proselytize.

7 Ancients and Moderns

Leo Strauss joined Carl Schmitt and Alexandre Kojève in their critiques of liberalism and liberal institutions. He shared their fear of world government. Strauss joined Hannah Arendt in her regard for the Greek *polis*, in her fears for modernity, and in her conviction that philosophy, especially the philosophy of fifth-century Athens, could invigorate not only modern philosophy but American democracy. Like most Europeans of a certain age, Strauss had contempt for mass culture, especially in its American form. He placed these critiques of modernity so vigorously before his students that some of the Straussians began to condemn the Moderns, and modernity, altogether. "But Mr. Strauss," a student asked, "Aren't *we* Moderns?" "Yes," Strauss is said to have responded, "but we are not *merely* Moderns."

At about the same time, in another part of the world, another theorist placed a similar set of critiques before his students and colleagues. Sayyid Qutb joined Hassan al Banna, leader of the Muslim Brothers, and Ruhollah Khomeini, a poet and scholar who was to craft the Iranian Revolution and a new Iranian constitution, in their critiques of liberal institutions. He joined Khomeini in his regard for the Koran as a design for a good political regime, in his fears for modernity, and in the conviction that the Koran could invigorate modern Islamic thought and politics.

At dinner some months ago, the sociologist Gershon Shafir told me that he thinks that the world is currently divided between the followers of Leo Strauss and the followers of Sayyid Qutb. This observation has insights and ironies worth exploring. The followers of Strauss stand in the advance guard of those directing the wars in Iraq and Afghanistan. The followers of Sayyid Qutb, their rivals and allies, stand in the advance guard of those who fought in Afghanistan. Most of those who have set themselves in opposition to the West, and many of those engaged in violent attacks on Western targets, see themselves as followers of Sayyid Qutb. They are, they believe, engaged in a struggle of more than worldly significance. The followers of Strauss see themselves symmetrically: standing for the defense of the West, for the revival of ancient teachings and a lost morality.

Sayyid Qutb's views were tempered, like Strauss's, in the fire of history. He was imprisoned and finally executed under Egyptian President Gamal Abdel Nasser. Before his death he had been extensively tortured. He lived under conditions of persecution, yet wrote quite openly of the moral and political failures of a regime he regarded as godless and corrupt. Qutb was, like Strauss, a teacher. He came from a small town in Egypt and began as a teacher and inspector of schools. He was sent to school in the United States in the late 1940s. Perhaps those who sent him sensed his growing opposition to the Egyptian government. Perhaps they thought that experience of the United States would broaden his intellectual horizons. If so, they were thoroughly mistaken. Qutb was sent to a small teaching college in Colorado. I suspect that he may be that college's most famous alumnus. The small Western town managed to thoroughly shock the Egyptian teacher who had seen Cairo, the city called *umm ad-dunya*, "mother of the world." Qutb returned to Egypt a confirmed critic of the West. He joined the Muslim Brothers, the *Ikwan al muslimmin*, wrote a series of books, and became one of the principal architects of modern Islamic radicalism. Qutb is read among the Muslim Brothers. He is read by people like Osama bin Laden's second in command, Ayman al Zawahiri, who joined the Muslim Brothers at fifteen and participated with al Qaeda in planning the attacks of 9/11. He is read by Western professors, including the political theorists Paul Berman and Roxanne Euben. Qutb is read, perhaps more important, by ordinary people around the world. I was given one of his books for free on a London street corner.

Qutb's writings, read straightforwardly, will please no one

completely—least of all his most fervent disciples. *Social Justice in Islam* supports women working outside the home and criticizes the ostensible "liberation" of women not for their entry into the public sphere, nor for licentiousness, but for the prevalence of sexual harassment in the workplace. He observes that when leaders drink Evian while most of the people lack clean water, religion and politics demand that the regime be reformed. He writes that mineral and other natural resources—oil, for example—are a common patrimony, and that wealth derived from these should be not be confined to a few. Qutb defends private property rights, and like most political Islamists (Muhammad was a merchant) favors trade and commerce. The institution of *zakat*, a Koranic requirement that is central to *Social Justice in Islam*, is to provide for the few who are permanently disabled and the many who are temporarily in financial difficulties without diminishing their dignity, by giving them the means for productive work. Qutb is, in short, a profoundly interesting theorist worth reading not merely as an exhibit in the archives of terror but for his comments on justice and forms of government.

Qutb's most zealous disciples have been more interested in other aspects of his work. In the years after 9/11 Qutb has been described as "the man who inspired bin Laden" and as a teacher of terrorists. The vision of governance advanced by Qutb is significantly different from that favored by Osama bin Laden, but the attribution is not entirely in error. Qutb appears to have inspired many in the ranks of militant Islam, Ayman al Zawahiri among them. He is most known in the Muslim world and among his disciples not for advocating armed attacks on the West but for permitting armed attacks by Muslims on Muslims. Qutb's fiercest opposition was reserved for corrupt regimes at home: for leaders violating the moral and political principles of Islam.

The world of Islam, like that of Christianity, has known civil war, and has seen a once-unified religion divided by internal conflict. Sunni and Shia have engaged in persecuting one another with a zeal almost equaling that of Protestant and Catholic. Qutb revived the study of Ahmad ibn Taymiyya, a philosopher active during the Mongol invasions. Ibn Taymiyya wrote that though the invading Mongols were Muslim, they could be fought because they did not fulfill the requirements of the faith. Sayyid Qutb argued that the same could be said of corrupt regimes in the (at least nominally) Muslim world. Sayyid Qutb's followers were first feared not for the threat they posed to the West but for the threat they posed to Arab and Muslim regimes.

Ironically, it may be this very inwardness that has brought the disciples of Sayyid Qutb into conflict with the followers of Leo Strauss. They opposed their regimes and were put into prison. Some were executed. Those who remained went underground and into exile. Sent away from nations, they made common cause with one another and established communities—and cells—in exile. Placed beyond national boundaries, they no longer confined themselves to national politics. They found themselves in the theater of a larger war. The prize was no longer Egypt but the world.

Before America became an empire Walt Whitman wrote:

Long yet your road, oh flag, and lined with bloody death.
For the prize I see at issue is the world.

Exile and ambition, persecution and a sense of mission, created a confrontation between the disciples of Qutb and the disciples of Strauss that was initially alien to the imaginations of both parties. The disciples of Sayyid Qutb saw themselves cleansing Egypt and the Muslim world, driving out "Pharoah." The disciples of Leo Strauss saw themselves as the salvation of modernity, restoring at least some of the strength and virtues that belonged to the Ancients. They thought they would make a home for philosophy in America. If each party had claimed, among its own, that the prize that was at issue was the world, no one would have believed them.

The critique of modernity current among the Straussians and their conservative allies bears a family resemblance to the critique current among Qutb's disciples and their allies. Each set of disciples has seen the modern world as corrosive of public and private virtue. Each has condemned modernity for nihilism. Both longed for a single standard of conduct for all. Each has displayed a distaste for mass culture and a distrust of mass politics. Both condemned totalitarianism in general and communism in particular.

Though their followers—and their critics—have often cast them as opposed to modernity, neither Strauss nor Qutb campaigned for a return to the purity of an imagined past. They saw dangers in modernity, especially liberal modernity, but they were not blind to modernity's virtues and possibilities. Their disciples would turn to more theatrical forms of ancestor worship. The disciples of Qutb grew beards, changed their costumes, and painted their eyes with kohl. They cultivated a romantic view of the time of the Prophet. The Straussians cultivated the romance of the Ancients.

For many of the Straussians, the Ancients are what they were to British poets and schoolboys of the nineteenth century. They are brave and blond and wise, living in a city of public assemblies and white marble temples, the Athens of the imagination. Once, when I was in college, one of my teachers was singing the praises of the Greeks to me and came in his panegyric to the pristine whiteness of their temples. "Well, they weren't," I said, firmly. "What?" he asked, his elegy interrupted. "They weren't white," I said, and told him, to his astonished dismay, of the vivid horizontal stripes of gold and red and blue that once enlivened the pristine marble temples of the Greeks.

As this suggests, the Straussians often seem strangely blind to the Ancients they read so carefully. They read the *Apology* and condemn homosexuality. They read Strauss on Aristophanes, yet they seem to miss a set of jokes as scatological as anything in Monty Python or *South Park*. They must have missed the part where Socrates gazes up to the heavens and a lizard defecates in his mouth. They read the *Bacchae* and the *Oresteia*, yet they picture the Greeks as resolutely Apollonian: restrained, virtuous, and lawful (if not always democratic). In these plays I see other, wilder Greeks. Agave runs through the woods with a pack of women, intoxicated with wine and Dionysos. She rips her son apart in a frenzy. As she holds his severed head in her hands, thinking that she has killed a dangerous lion, her father says, "When you realize the horror you have done you will suffer terribly. But if with luck your present madness lasts until you die, you will seem to have, not having, happiness." Agamemnon sacrifices his daughter Iphigenia, binding her mouth so that he will not hear her cries. Euripides wrote of Hecuba, the queen of Troy, when she was queen no longer. In the play, Hecuba is an exile and a slave. She says to the Greek commander Odysseus, "And you have power Odysseus, greatness and power. But clutch them gently, use them kindly, for power gives no purchase to the hand, it will not hold, soon perishes, and greatness goes. I know, I once was great, but I am nothing now. One day cut down my greatness and my pride." There is much they might hear in these texts, but the Straussians keep to the Greeks of their imagination.

The Athens of the Straussian imagination, pure and white, inhabited by the wise and blond, was the home of Socrates, the individual, standing alone against the city, obedient to its laws. Straussians had an imagined modernity as well. Modernity was the movement of masses: mass politics, mass culture, a force against which no man could stand alone. Modernity set convention, the unconscious power of the mass, against law, against tradition, against reason. Modernity made man—one man that might be any man—the measure of all things. Modernity saw not only the *Götterdämmerung*, the death of the gods, but the death of God.

In modernity, people left the ordered hierarchy of traditional life. They abandoned a world of distinctions for a world of uniformities. The modern world was a world of mass manufacture in which craftsmanship had disappeared. It was a world of mass politics and mass society in which people were only that, individuals, recognizing no hierarchies, no distinctions. The death of god and the decline of distinction were the deaths of excellence and virtue. People resolved themselves into a mass, and—as a mass—they were small, indeterminate, and contemptible.

If modernity was bad, postmodernity is worse. Moderns made man the measure of all things. Postmodernity took that measure into many. Postmodernity, even more than modernity, was the moment of the mass. Man had killed god, in the modernity of the Straussian imagination; in postmodernity, the last moment of modernity, man would kill that face of god which was the *logos*. *Logos* is a Greek term dear to the Straussians, for it conflates order, law, meaning, and the word. The *logos* might be law or scripture, the word of god, or the constitutional order. Postmodernity argued that law, meaning, and the word were made in practice and over time, that those who lived under laws, read books, used words, and lived in constitutional orders took part in making them. Straussians feared nihilism, the absence of meaning. In modernity, they lost the guidance of a single standard. Postmodernity was the last, the final, the ultimate moment of modernity. The single standard, one common to all human beings, had broken into many. Cultural relativism answered the demands of divided humanity. Modernity spoke to the needs of the masses, postmodernity to their desires. The last moment of modernity was the moment of the Last Man: soft. Nihilism, cultural relativism, and the Last Man are linked in the Straussian imagination. They are linked in Strauss's work as well.

Strauss wrote several books. They are quite different from one another. For the Straussians, though not for the students of Strauss, one book seems to stand apart from the rest. *Natural Right and History* casts America as the site of an escape from history, the chance for modernity to be something more than merely modern. This book casts America as the site of modernity's redemption. In doing so, Strauss is following in the footsteps of Hegel. Hegel argued that history moves West. Mankind has its birth in the East, its youth in Greece, its maturity in Europe. America, removed from Europe by a great sea, is outside history. America is the realm of an uncertain future. Because America was beyond history, America might offer an escape from this historical epoch: an escape from modernity.

For Strauss, the means for that escape were captured in America's adherence to natural rights. The Declaration of Independence, honored by all Americans, declared, "We hold these truths to be self-evident, that all men are created equal, that they are endowed by their Creator with certain unalienable Rights, that among these are Life, Liberty, and the pursuit of Happiness." This affirmation of faith in natural rights did more than merely survive in the Declaration, it is known to every schoolchild.

Reading the Declaration of Independence as an affirmation of faith in natural rights could be a rallying cry. It could embolden people to seize their own rights or defend the rights of others. When Martin Luther King recalled the language of the Declaration in his speech at the Lincoln Memorial, it was in this way: to call Americans back to their revolutionary commitments. For Tom Paine, in the American and French Revolutions natural rights were the Rights of Man, and they were used to affirm the rights of the common people against kings and aristocrats. For Jefferson, for those who signed (and those who still affirm) the Declaration, governments are obliged to secure these rights. Natural rights necessitate that governments have the consent of the governed. Rights are the end of government, and a limit on it. Democratic governments are founded on these rights. They must secure them and—as the Bill of Rights would affirm a few years later—they cannot violate them. Natural rights, understood in this way, lead to a vigorous democracy.

The rights of the Declaration—to life, liberty, and the pursuit of happiness—are rights made to grow. People with these rights move outward. They move freely in the world, living longer, wider lives. They gather property, they pursue their happiness as they choose. They grow larger, ruling more, owning more, pursuing more, and their rights grow with them. In *Natural Right and History*, natural rights are used differently. They are the means not for extending democracy but for limiting it. In this reading, natural rights present an alternative to the consent of the governed. They limit what people can do, not only in their relations with others but for themselves. They are constrained in every direction. Natural right is necessary, Strauss tells us, to furnish "a standard with reference to which we can distinguish between genuine needs and fancied needs." Strauss writes in *Natural Right and History* that "the contemporary rejection of natural right leads to nihilism, nay it is identical with nihilism." By returning to natural rights, Moderns might escape some of modernity's dangers.

Nihilism is much feared, but it does not seem to be very fearsome. There may not be any nihilists at all. The successful nihilist, able to destroy meaning altogether, to produce a moral and intellectual chaos in which anything might mean anything else, seems a rare animal indeed. If one were to appear, it seems likely that we would take nihilism for madness—if we understood it at all. For Straussians, for Strauss in *Natural Right and History*, the world is full of nihilists. Not only those much-feared poststructuralists, postmodernists, and cultural relativists, but anyone who rejects natural right must be a nihilist. The passage from *Natural Right and History* suggests what they might mean by this accusation, why nihilism seems so common, why it troubles them, and why it need not trouble us.

Natural right offers a single standard for a single nature. But does man have a single nature?

In his exchanges with Kojève, Strauss suggests otherwise. People may be alike in their first nature, they may have their animal, bodily, nature in common, but this first nature is supplemented by others, and it is through these, as these, in these other natures that people come to politics and philosophy.

We are human, but to say that is to say only a little more than "we are animals." We eat, we need food and shelter. We can kill, and we are in danger of death from others. The little more in us leads from first to second nature. That which is second nature to an Athenian is not second nature to a Spartan. That which is second nature to an Orthodox Jew may not be second nature to a fundamentalist Christian, a Buddhist, or an atheist. If the standard is to address only our first nature, then perhaps one is enough. One standard will not, however, be enough for politics, or for philosophy.

Anyone who acknowledges the presence of different standards, the possibility of different forms of moral life, the need to weigh the actions of different people by different standards, is called a nihilist by these anxious men. If we do not all hold to the same standard, they argue, all meaning will be in peril. Without a single standard, anything goes. But does it? When have we all held to a single standard in America? Jefferson believed in natural rights, Hamilton did not. Both crafted the regime. Puritan divines, Shakers, Quakers, priests, and rabbis looked to the word of

God, but they held to different standards for justice, conduct, virtue, and politics.

We do not, it seems, believe that we need to hold all people to the same standard of judgment; and with good reason. Few of us would hold a child to the standard of an adult. Few of us would argue that the performance of a president and that of an athlete should be measured by the same standard. Our ordinary practices tell us that different occupations, different needs, demand different standards. Like the cook who knows that flour and milk should not be measured by the same cup, who uses a teaspoon and a tablespoon, a pound and a pint, we have no horror of using different measures. Good bread cannot be made without them.

The term "nihilism" is misleading here, and that is part of the trouble. The word suggests that those who recognize the presence of different standards for different forms of moral life annihilate meaning. For these, the deconstructionists, poststructuralists, existentialists, cultural relativists, multiculturalists, all meaning has been lost. There is nothing left: no virtue, no ethics, no guidance. They have no demands to meet, and no standards to satisfy. Anything goes. Yet when we look more closely, something seems amiss. These are the same people the Straussians castigate for political correctness, for enforcing demands of civility that are too rigid and too unyielding, standards of conduct that are too difficult to satisfy. The world of the nihilists has more meaning rather than less. Their world—our world—has in it not only the species being of Marx, in which all are alike, and the single standard by which all—being alike—are to be measured. Their world has the Americans and the French, the child and the citizen, the priest, the rabbi, the soldier, the farmer, the philosopher. They have not only their first nature to consider, but their second natures as well. They are obliged to think more of themselves. They are obliged to think more of others. The Straussians (though not only the Straussians) say the unexamined life is not worth living. The desire for a single standard, always the same in every age, is the desire to live an unexamined life. If there is a single standard, there is no need to ask what one is measuring, what qualities one is judging, what standard is appropriate.

Strauss saw, as Nietzsche had before him, hazards in the softness and civility of modern life. The aim of that life was, as Thomas Hobbes had argued in the midst of the English Civil War, a defense from enemies outside, and peace within the state, individuals justly and not extravagantly enriched by their own labor, and the enjoyment of freedom in the ordinary course of life. Such a life, as Nietzsche, Schmitt, Strauss, and Kojève feared, was a life of small pleasures and small ambition, few risks and few achievements, few dangers and little greatness of soul. The old virtues of courage and daring would be lost. People bred to so quiet a life would be as cats are to tigers, tamed and diminished.

This was civilization. This was the work of politics: the creation of a civil order in which politics itself might come to an end. This was the place of the comfort-loving Last Man. It is common for Straussians, and many other intellectuals, to inveigh against the Last Man. The Last Man likes radio, television, and all forms of mass entertainment, as long as they aren't too intellectual. The Last Man likes simple comforts. Those of us with shallower roots in the academy might find that this description strikes a little too close to home. You may have already recognized that the Last Man of Nietzsche is also the Last Man of Garrison Keillor and (in another vein) David Sedaris. The Last Man likes mashed potatoes and gravy, macaroni and cheese, brownies and ice cream. The Last Man takes his kids to McDonald's for the Happy Meal. The Last Man and (let us be fair) the Last Woman live with the Last Kids and the Last Dog (unquestionably a Labrador) in the suburbs. Because they want to feel safe and like to be comfortable, they drive an SUV with automatic transmission. They go to church and synagogue and watch *Oprah* and CNN.

The Last Man is Harry Truman as well as Homer Simpson. He still works, despite the end of history, and worries about his children's college tuition, and credit card debt. Thurber understands him as well as (perhaps a good deal better than) Nietzsche does. So did J. R. R. Tolkien. *The Lord of the Rings* makes the salvation of the world rest not simply on the great deeds of great men and the work of the wise, but on the courage and sacrifice, the generosity and the fortitude of ordinary people. Tolkien knew the hobbits as his countrymen; I know the Last Man and the Last Woman very well myself. I have known them all my life.

Those people called "the greatest generation" were, for the most part, Last Men and Last Women. They went to a necessary war, a war they judged just. They went mindful of their small comforts, taking pleasure in packages sent from home, and they did great things. When they returned, they went back to simple lives. Some (more than ever before) went to college on the G.I. Bill. They worked hard. They built suburbs and strip malls. They and the children they raised made the great reforms of the civil rights movement. They voted justice into law. They made the world Hobbes had hoped to make. They were defended from enemies outside the state. They were justly and not extravagantly enriched by their own labor. They sought the enjoyment of freedom in the ordinary course of life for themselves, for their people, and for their posterity.

Democracies are made of ordinary people who will take on the burdens of greatness at need, and of the great and the wise willing to set greatness aside. The ordinary citizen, called to war, asked to board the landing craft to Normandy or the bus to Selma, takes greatness up. The brilliant are asked to set greatness aside in the voting booth and the grocery line, to live quietly. They are able to do this because they see the potential for greatness in those they join. Democracy has taught them that honor is greater than glory.

8 The Statesman

Political Straussians are great admirers of civil religion. They are pious practitioners as well, and have both secular saints and a series of rituals. The most conspicuous among those saints are Winston Churchill and Abraham Lincoln. Those Straussians holding positions of power and influence advance other exemplars of leadership, Lee Kuan Yew of Singapore and General Pervez Musharraf of Pakistan among them. We need to ask which leaders they honor, and why they honor them, to see the forms of leadership they advocate for America.

Winston Churchill is admired by many Americans as the leader of a determined British resistance to Nazi Germany. That determination was expressed most vividly for these admirers in the famous exhortation after Dunkirk. "We shall not flag nor fail. We shall go on to the end, we shall fight in France, we shall fight on the seas and oceans, we shall fight with growing confidence and growing strength in the air, we shall defend our Island, whatever the cost may be, we shall fight on the beaches, we shall fight on the landing grounds, we shall fight in the fields and in the streets, we shall fight in the hills; we shall never surrender." Churchill did that which he called on all Britons to do. "Let us therefore brace ourselves to our duties, and so bear ourselves that if the British Empire and Commonwealth last for a thousand years, men will still say, This was their finest hour." And so they do. For Americans who came of age during the Second World War and shortly after, Churchill represented intrepid and beleaguered Britain. He represented the British of Dunkirk and the Blitz, steadfast in the face of adversity. The British were, like Tolkien's hobbits, a small people capable of great things, beloved for their warm houses, simple pleasures, and unsuspected fortitude.

Churchill's Straussian admirers go beyond this. Churchill embodies to them, as he does to others, opposition to peculiarly modern tyrannies. He is honored as the opponent of totalitarianism in the Soviet Union as well as in Nazi Germany. Here, as elsewhere one sees the affinities between the students of Strauss and the students of Arendt, for it is Arendt's understanding of totalitarianism that is at work. Churchill is admirable because he opposes totalitarianism in both of its manifestations, Eastern and Western, Nazi and Communist.

There are other aspects of Churchill, aspects that explain the postwar rejection of his government that seems so inexplicable to

Americans. Churchill was not merely the defender of that "emerald island set in a silver sea," the champion of a nation of valiant hobbits. He was also the defender of an aging empire, unwilling to let go of an indefensible form of rule. He was the opponent of the working class. He held on to a decaying feudalism at home and abroad.

In this American retelling of British history, all Churchill's vices turn to virtues. Churchill is Frodo, standing valiantly against the Dark Lord, holding fast to an England of green fields, small farms, and country pleasures. If this entailed a rejection of industrial modernity, so much the better. It is not the England of George Eliot, of slow starvation, pawned overcoats, and broken strikes, that Americans regard with nostalgia. Americans, especially American conservatives, have a tendency to forget their own origins when they think of England. They forget the empire, or rather, they remember it in sepia and Technicolor. They remember the Raj of Kipling and *Masterpiece Theatre*, of crisp linen suits and solar topees, of polo matches and cucumber sandwiches. They forget the Amritsar massacre, Churchill's slurs at Gandhi, and the long indifference to the rights of man in Ireland. For them, Churchill stands less for the might of the Raj than for the valor of Dunkirk.

In the world Churchill represents, men live in the warm light of custom. They have power and they use it well. They have inferiors, and they serve them well. The costs of unearned privilege, the burdens of hierarchy, are bathed in that roseate glow. The figure of Churchill enables latter-day imperialists to represent empire in the guise of the underdog. The England of Dunkirk and the Blitz veils the England that breaks the coal miners' strike, starves the Irish, and rules the empire. American admiration for Churchill is commonly admiration for an England stripped of empire, returned to its ancient boundaries and ancient virtues. Churchill's attachment to a world of inherited privilege, of wealth and ancestry, can be forgotten because he has joined the commons.

The second of the Straussian secular saints is an honored and especially malleable figure in American politics, Abraham Lincoln. For many scholars, especially among the Straussians, the malleability of Lincoln's memory points not to a defect in national recollection but to the first of Lincoln's virtues. Lincoln is the model of prudential leadership. Some Straussians go further in their use of Lincoln—further than most Americans would be willing to follow them. This is the case with Carnes Lord's *The Modern Prince: What Leaders Need to Know Now*.

Carnes Lord's book is of special interest here because it presents itself as a study of statesmanship. Written by a Straussian, it is praised by Harvey Mansfield, by William Kristol, and by Fred Iklé, a former undersecretary of defense in the Reagan administration. Here, it appears, is a work on statesmanship endorsed by both academic and political Straussians. If the Straussians intend to act as leaders, or merely to advise them, we would do well to know what they think a good leader, a good statesman, ought to be. We need to consider not only how and why they honor Lincoln and Churchill, but who else they put in their company, what they say of statesmanship, and where they think it leads.

The Modern Prince is, of course, modeled on Machiavelli's famous (or perhaps infamous) work *The Prince*. Machiavelli would not have minded the imitation, for, as he observes, it is a good idea for a man to imitate his betters "so that, if his own ingenuity does not come up to theirs, at least it will have the smell of it." (He was more tolerant than Hobbes, who noted that men often "stick their corrupt doctrines with the cloves of other men's wit.") Machiavelli is, however, a surprising model for a Straussian in other respects. One of Strauss's most famous works was *Thoughts on Machiavelli*, and in that work Strauss writes that Machiavelli was "a teacher of evil."

The Modern Prince follows the pattern of praise for Churchill and Lincoln, but uses it as a warrant for a more troubling model of leadership. Churchill is "by common consent, the greatest statesman of the twentieth century." Lincoln is the preserver of Union and democracy, an accomplishment arguably more difficult than founding a state. Praise for these is, however, joined to praise for others, for the "considerable courage" of Pervez Musharraf and the "unapologetic" elitism of Lee Kuan Yew. Lee is the model of that form of leadership praised by Lord in his chapter on autocratic democracy.

Pervez Musharraf is, of course, the Pakistani general and head of state. His "considerable courage" was shown in the wake of

9/11 when he agreed to collaborate with the United States in the invasion of Afghanistan. It is rather generous of Lord to call this courage. With the United States declaring war on terror and inveighing against the evils of nuclear proliferation, Musharraf might have thought he was in the American gun sights. This was, after all, the same Pervez Musharraf whose regime had tolerated the training of terrorists for al Qaeda operations in madrasas throughout Pakistan, who had furnished protection and assistance to violent insurgents in Kashmir, and who had expanded his country's nuclear arsenal and aimed it at India, a vibrantly democratic nation. Under these circumstances, one might regard Musharraf's actions as motivated less by courage than by a desperate attempt at survival. It was Musharraf, moreover, who airlifted Taliban out of the reach of American forces and gave them refuge in Pakistan, and Musharraf who continued to protect the paramilitary madrasas and Kashmiri militants after the fall of the Taliban. Musharraf is also responsible for the spread of nuclear technology to Iran. It was on Musharraf's watch that A. Q. Khan conveyed Pakistani nuclear expertise, technology, and material to the Iranian nuclear weapons program. A generous person might class these as sins of omission; a skeptical one might regard them as double-dealing. We are no safer and he is no better for it.

Musharraf is, in plain language, a military dictator. Is it good policy to have those who teach our nation's officers praising military dictators?

Lee Kuan Yew is praised similarly. He has, Lord tells us, kept his country firmly aligned with the United States. He has kept Singapore free from the influences of communism and socialism. Yew believed that these ideologies might have proved popular among some Singaporeans. We'll never know. They were, as Lord observes approvingly, firmly repressed. Lord praises Lee not only for resisting communism and socialism (at the cost of democracy) but for his resistance to "Western (and particularly American) liberalism." Liberalism here seems to refer to that of Locke, for what Lee (and Lord) object to is an emphasis on rights and the individual.

Lord's enthusiasm for Lee does not extend to his culture or his people. Southeast Asia is the realm of "cronyism and corruption." Lee was shaped instead by "early exposure to the values and procedures of parliamentary democracy in the English mode." Lee is good not as a Southeast Asian but as one who has become an Englishman, and remade his nation accordingly. That Lee has "enjoyed virtually absolute control of the Singaporean parliament since the 1960s" ought not to sway our judgment of this eminently English polity. One might, however, stop to wonder: which England? The England of Blair? Of Burke? Or perhaps the England of Dickens, Eliot, and Disraeli's *Coningsby*?

The praise of Lee Kuan Yew as an "unapologetic elitist" suggests that the admiration for Churchill among the Straussians is not quite coincident with the broader American regard for Churchill. The praise of Lincoln becomes questionable as well.

Is the Lincoln praised here the Great Emancipator or the Lincoln who suspended habeas corpus? Does Lord wish us to admire setting the Constitution aside in favor of martial law?

The answer *The Modern Prince* gives to the latter question is an unqualified yes. Lord is critical of nations that reverence their constitutions. The book's closing chapter criticizes those nations, especially democracies, where the constitution is so strong that "it seems to be hewn out of a kind of political granite that is hard to topple and highly resistant to erosion." Lincoln urged Americans to teach their youngest children reverence for the Constitution. Lord praises him for setting it aside. *The Modern Prince* values most highly those leaders willing to take on dictatorial powers, to rule for some period not as democratic but as authoritarian leaders. Lincoln is valued here not for his faith in the Constitution, for freeing the slaves, or for prudence simply understood, but because he presents seemingly irrefutable evidence of the virtue of dictatorial action on behalf of democracy. He thus belongs with Lee Kuan Yew, Atatürk, and Pervez Musharraf, rather than with Washington, Mandela, and those few others who refused authority for the sake of the national democracy. The moral force of Lincoln's work against slavery provides the warrant for a more authoritarian presidency.

When I was at Chicago, there were two speeches read by virtually all students in the Common Core: Pericles' Funeral Oration and Lincoln's Gettysburg Address. One of our classmates famously confused the two and—more famously—appealed the rather bad grade he got in consequence on the grounds that, after all, they were very much the same. A similar sentiment seems to animate Lord's study of statesmanship, in which Pericles is mistaken for Lincoln. Lord praises Lincoln as an autocrat in the defense of democracy. His praise of Pericles places democracy in the autocrat's service. The chapter on autocratic democracy begins with Thucydides' judgment that Periclean Athens was a democracy in name only, an autocracy in fact, and continues with praise of modern autocratic leaders. Throughout the work the reader is told that leaders must to learn how to "manage" elites. Leadership, in this view, is not a matter of using advisers well, as Reagan was said to do. Still less is it a matter of consultation. Leadership is autocracy.

A generous reader might offer, in Lord's defense, that Atatürk regarded himself as shepherding Turkey from the sultanate to more democratic forms of rule. He was a dictator, he declared, so that Turkey might never have another. Lee seems to see his work in similar terms. Lord's book is addressed, however, not to the subjects of sultans, autocrats, and dictators but to Americans. Americans have learned that backing autocrats abroad is a bad strategy. The Shah of Iran was our autocrat. When he fell, blame for his secret police, his reliance on torture, and his silencing of dissent fell on us as well. Saudi Arabia has been so closely allied with the United States that my colleague Robert Vitalis calls it "America's kingdom." When the planes hit the World Trade Center, several of the hijackers were Saudi. So is Osama bin Laden. History as well as ethics would suggest that backing autocrats is a bad business. The violence of our chosen autocrats comes home to us.

Only the innocent "bourgeois democrat," accustomed to democracy, will, Lord writes, quibble with his praise of the autocratic modernizing of Atatürk and Lee Kuan Yew. America, however, still listens to the innocent democrats of its middle class. We are the people the autocrat would rule. Lord's vision of leadership does not keep autocracy abroad, it brings autocracy home.

Good leaders, Lord argues, not only manage elites autocratically, they rule education autocratically as well. Schools are not simply places for learning. The leader should intervene actively to promote civic morality. The teaching of civic morality is, of course, impossible to avoid, even should one wish to do so. The standards of conduct held by a given people emerge in who they honor, and why they honor them, the holidays they observe, and the (often quite varied) histories they read. Lord has something more active in mind. Civic morality is not to emerge, with as little hindrance as possible, from the practices, thought, reflection, and debate of a people over time, directed by parents, teachers, authors, local school boards, and the sense of the community in practice. Instead, it is to be directed by the government, more precisely by the particular leaders in power. "Political leaders have every right to form and express judgments about the teaching of national history, and to take action to shape public school curriculums in this area." Nor should universities be (as another civic morality taught) places of unhindered learning and free speech. On the contrary, universities should be held "politically accountable" for leftist professors and other "lunatic and sinister" faculty. They should be required to track students for the federal government.

What would this entail? The truth squads that once roamed the halls of Chicago would have a broader, and more official, mandate. Like the enforcers of virtue in Iran who roam the streets, looking for the woman whose veil has slipped and shown a lock of hair, whose chador is not quite large enough, Lord's moral police, his American *basiji*, would be on the prowl. With each classroom once open to any opinion, however errant, with free speech a common practice, it would be necessary to exercise constant and intense vigilance. There are, Lord tells us, no small number of leftists, "lunatic and sinister" professors, and not all of them are visible. They would have to be identified. All classes would have to be supervised, and, out of class, books and articles checked to ensure that their opinions were neither lunatic nor sinister. These books and articles would have to accord with the standards set by the leader, for it is the leader's right and responsibility to shape the teaching of history and morality, and to use political power to this end. If we are to protect ourselves from danger, then we must track foreign students, or any students who might pose a threat to national security. How are they to be found? Here too, vigilance would be required. Perhaps students of a certain ethnicity, or students who study certain languages, or students who chose certain books to read or classes to take might be examined first. Their meetings would also have to be supervised.

Perhaps education is a special case, and Lord's morals police and American *basiji* would confine themselves to schools and the universities. Perhaps the constant supervision of opinions, the always-present, always-listening ear of the state, would be open only to teachers and students. Perhaps the recording of what is written and read, who meets with whom, and where and for what purpose, who travels abroad and where and why and with whom they meet, would be confined to the universities. Perhaps not.

Lord provides two justifications for the leader's autocratic encroachments on ordinary liberties. The first is contained in his final chapter, "Exhortation to Preserve Democracy from the Barbarians." We are threatened by the Chinese, the Muslims, multiculturalists, and "unassimilated minorities." Who then are "we"? The Hasids of Brooklyn and Bala Cynwyd and the rambunctious family of *My Big Fat Greek Wedding* are enemy aliens in Lord's vision of America. The Amish, speaking plattdeutsch and making shoo-fly pie in Pennsylvania, and the "trouble-making professoriate" are all "barbarians." Lord's second justification for autocracy is now more familiar than it once was. Each of us must give up our freedoms so that we all can be safe. Homeland security requires it. Patriotism is the reason for the sacrifice of freedom.

No justification could be more ironic than these. Machiavelli's final chapter is titled "Exhortation to Take Hold of Italy and

Liberate Her from the Barbarians." In it Machiavelli calls upon his countrymen to liberate themselves from the unwelcome rule of a foreign invader. Lord writes in support of those who have made themselves foreign invaders and unwelcome rulers.

Strauss, however, explicitly rejected this aspect of Machiavelli. "To justify Machiavelli's terrible counsels by having recourse to his patriotism, means to see the virtues of that patriotism while being blind to that which is higher than patriotism or to that which both hallows and limits patriotism." Patriotism was a suspect virtue for Strauss. This should hardly surprise us. The experience of Germany in the 1930s might well lead one to suspect any appeal to patriotism alone. Patriotism, Strauss reminds us, can easily be used "to obscure something truly evil." But Strauss would have had stronger objections to Lord's appropriation of Machiavelli. "The United States of America," Strauss wrote, was "the only country in the world founded in explicit opposition to Machiavellian principles." While other countries ruled by force, "by the sword," in the United States, Strauss argued, it was not possible to clothe "public and private gangsterism" in the garb of patriotism. Lord holds to a less exacting standard. He has no qualms about recommending duplicity and autocratic rule to the modern leader. He is a professor of strategy at the Naval War College.

Another reading of Machiavelli holds that *The Prince* was written not for the prince but for the people. The people would see the depredations, the conniving, the cruelty of princes as Machiavelli laid these before them. The people would hear when Machiavelli declared that a people who had once been free never lost the memory of their liberty. Machiavelli wrote: "Whoever becomes master of a city accustomed to living in freedom and does not destroy it may expect to be destroyed by it; because this city can always have refuge, during a rebellion, in the name of liberty and its traditional institutions, neither of which, with the passing of time or the conferring of benefits, are ever forgotten." Behind the exhortation addressed to the prince to free his people from foreign rule was another addressed to the people. Machiavelli called on them to free themselves from the rule of princes, to remember Rome of the Republic, to recall their ancient liberty and laws, and take government into their hands again.

Remembering our ancient liberty, our law, and our own republic, we might come to a different view of "what modern leaders need to know." We might remember that passage in which Machiavelli instructs leaders to put their faith in the common people rather than in elites. Elites, he argued, wish to oppress, the people wish only to avoid oppression. We might decide that preserving the republic and our own liberty is work not for our leaders but for ourselves.

9 On Tyranny

In the year 2001, in the wake of September 11, the United States government began a war that was not a war. The war was said to be against terror and terrorism. Terror and terrorism in Ireland, Sri Lanka, and Kashmir went untouched. The forces of the United States advanced on Afghanistan in pursuit of Osama bin Laden. They never found the man who had launched the attacks of 9/11, though they deposed the regime that had sheltered him. Later a larger force invaded and occupied Iraq, searching perhaps for a link to these attackers, perhaps for weapons of mass destruction. There was no link to al Qaeda. There were no weapons of mass destruction.

Prisoners without a nation were kept in a territory without a nation, outside the Constitution, outside the governance of the Geneva Convention, outside the requirements of American law, in Guantánamo Naval Base. Those captured in Afghanistan were termed "unlawful enemy combatants" rather than prisoners of war. They were brought to Guantánamo, in Cuba, rather than to the United States. Guantánamo is held under a long-term lease from Cuba which, by the terms of the treaty establishing it, could be terminated only with the consent of both parties. The United States, having refused to terminate the lease, officially regards the territory as outside American jurisdiction. Cuba, refusing to recognize the legitimacy of a lease it wishes to terminate, and unable to retake the territory, cannot bring the base within the reach of Cuban law. Guantánamo thus remains a no-man's-land, outside the easy reach of international law. Guantánamo, under American control but not under American jurisdiction, offered a space in which prisoners could be kept on those terms: within American control but not under American law.

As regimes fell, the Bush administration declared "mission accomplished" but let the nation know, quietly, obliquely, that the war would be a "long, hard slog" that might outlast our lifetimes. The newly created Department of Homeland Security declared that terrorists might strike anywhere, from anywhere, at any time. They might be from any country, even our own. The Department of Defense suggested that Syria and Lebanon, North Korea and Iran might be next in the gun sights of a preemptive strike. This was war without boundaries, war without limits.

When weapons of mass destruction were not confirmed by United Nations arms inspectors, President Bush declared that they were hidden. They posed an imminent threat. When weapons of mass destruction were not deployed, President Bush declared that decisive military action by the United States had precluded their use. When searches failed to find weapons of mass destruction, President Bush declared that there had been an imminent threat of their development. When evidence of their development could not be found, President Bush declared that the United States had acted "before an imminent threat" was posed.

The just-war theory of Augustine, Aquinas, and al Farabi had held that a nation could wage war justly if attacked, or if the threat of an attack was clear and imminent in the present. Neither acts in the past nor fears for the future could justify an unprovoked attack. If unprovoked attacks, based on past resentments and future fears were justified, who would be immune? What nation would be safe? If a nation could attack because it feared not that it might be attacked tomorrow or the next day, or the next month, but in some vague future, who would be immune? The future would be hostage not to actions but to fears, and the most fearful (if they were powerful enough) could wage war with impunity. Traditional just-war theory offers no defense for wars like these. When the threat lies in an uncertain future, and the enemy is unidentified, Augustine, Aquinas, and al Farabi would not permit a preemptive strike.

Straussians may prefer Ancients to Moderns, but the Ancients will not give them justifications for the wars they wage. The Ancients required an enemy, a clear threat, and an authority empowered to make war. The Moderns are as demanding. Despite the excesses of modern warfare, people continue to believe that first strikes require justification. Carl Schmitt, who founded politics on the distinction between friend and enemy, made it clear that a nation could make war legitimately only against an enemy that posed a "mortal threat." If it were to be a cause for war, the threat had to be not only mortal but clear and immediate. Ancients and Moderns, even at their most warlike, were concerned to maintain limits on war. The proponents of war without limits must find other justifications, other warrants for the wars they wage.

A defense of war without limits requires an account of danger in which threats continually change their shape and location. Curiously, some (though not all) of the materials necessary for this defense may come from those the Straussians most despise: the poststructuralists and their fellow travelers. Michael Hardt and Antonio Negri in *Empire* and Alfredo G. A. Valladão in *The Twenty-First Century Will Be American* all describe a global order in which the advice and actions of the Straussians of the Bush administration are entirely rational. The world, as they see it, is evolving into a global network. There is no longer a world of separate states, each with a center, each falling when the center is captured. Rather than thinking of power as a matter of center and periphery, centers and margins, we should see it as a network. This network of power covers the world. Power moves through that network, linking distant sites, able to operate in many places at once. There is no center. Attack what was once a center, Washington or New York, and watch. The government does not fall. Power is decentralized, diffused. The president is in Miami, the vice president is underground, and if they were to die, there would be others to take their places. Power operates like a grid. Should one part of the grid fail, power can flow to (and from) other parts. The federal government lapses, and the states come forward. This form of power may be at its most developed—its most ordinary—in the United States, but it describes a world beyond the United States, and beyond American control. Attack al Qaeda in Afghanistan and find cells in Hamburg, bomb the caves of Tora Bora and nightclubs are bombed in Bali.

Sovereignty moves in this form as well. Once, when there were kings, sovereignty was incarnate in the body of a man. Later, sovereignty pooled in governmental bodies, concentrated at the center of power, flowing outward from that center. Democracy reverses the flow. Sovereignty comes from the people, dispersed or assembled, and it moves not simply toward a single center but throughout the system in a constant flow. Sovereignty, authority, power move from the people to the center—to the capital, to the head of state, to the Constitution—and they also move to more local authorities: to states, counties, and towns, to school boards and local committees.

In the American republic, neither power nor sovereignty flows to a single center. Power flows from the people to Washington, but it also flows from the people to the state capitols at Harrisburg, Springfield, Albany, Sacramento. Authority flows to states and municipalities, to county courts and school boards as well as to the federal government. There is no center of power and authority here. Instead, there is a structure. Power and authority do not flow through the structure toward a center: power and authority animate the whole, from the township and school board to the Supreme Court, Congress, and the presidency. Sovereignty moves through the people, igniting the whole. Rousseau wrote, long before the founding of America, that the term "citizen" united subject and sovereign in a single word, subjection and sovereignty in a single citizen. The United States made that recognition live; Whitman made it poetry.

> One's-Self I sing, a simple separate person
> Yet utter the word Democratic, the word En-Masse.

Democracy, in Whitman's American view, was a state of profound uniformity, in the strict sense. The American democracy appeared wildly diverse. "I hear American singing, the varied carols I hear": the sounds of mason and carpenter, boatman and shoemaker, and, later, philosopher and president, prostitute and criminal. The surface of the democracy was shifting and varied, as various as the world it reflected, but beneath this surface diversity, there was a deep likeness. For Whitman, the American democracy was the world's future:

Any period one nation must lead

One land must be the promise and reliance of the future

These states are the amplest poem.

Here is not a nation but a teeming nation of nations.

The American democracy could accommodate all these because, fundamentally, at bottom, people were alike. They might be represented as leaves of grass, that "uniform hieroglyphic."

Whitman's poetic conception ("I am," he said, "the most venerable mother") united difference and uniformity in a common political vision. Whitman saw the wild diversity of individuals—their occupations, talents, sins, virtues, cities, states—rooted in a single humanity. For Whitman, this wild diversity was a source of pleasure, uniformity reason for hope. The European philosophers saw matters differently than did the American poet. For them, difference was the source of conflict, and uniformity a future to fear.

In the 1950s, in the midst of the Cold War, Leo Strauss and Alexandre Kojève, a French civil servant and scholar of Hegel, read a neglected dialogue of Xenophon, *Hiero; or, the Tyrant*. In the course of their reading, and their debate with each other, they took up the question of the end of history, and the emergence of the "universal and homogenous state." The specter of a world governed under a single authority, all differences erased, haunted the world between the wars. The League of Nations is remembered now for its lack of power, its weakness, its inefficiency. Strauss and Kojève saw in the League and other multi-national institutions the threat of an imperial totalitarianism: absorbing all. Nationals and peoples would disappear, the rich tapestry of European culture—indeed, of all the varied cultures of the world—would fade into uniformity.

Strauss, Schmitt, and Kojève feared the "universal and homogenous state" as the state of Nietzsche's Last Man, loving comfort, threatening no one, lacking a sense of gravity, seeking only entertainment. This same fear animates those students of Strauss who look to war to restore the manly virtues threatened by the end of history. They need have no fear. Power is a net in this unexpected future.

The state that has shown itself in our time is not the "universal and homogenous state" but a state of networked unity, complete with gaps, absences, and interruptions. The emergent future appeared to Strauss and Kojève as a condition of uninterrupted sovereignty and power. The emergent future appears to us as a net: a series of knots of nodes, separate and particular, bound ever more closely in their particularity. The metaphor of the net captures the postmodern condition of local loyalties made denser, local loyalties bound tighter. Nations and nationalism do not wither away, they generate. There are Slovenes and Bosnians, Serbs and Croats and Macedonians where there were once Yugoslavians. Where they once expected the triumph of the International, they have seen the triumph of older and smaller nationalisms. These are joined by more local loyalties, at once bound to and independent of their allies. Hezbollah in southern Lebanon is not Hezbollah in Turkey, and neither can be seen simply as a satellite of Iran. Yet Hezbollah or any radical Islamist organization may link itself to other radical Islamist organizations: in Chechnya or Egypt, Bali or Brixton. Amazonian tribes discuss strategies with Canada's First Nations, the Mayans in Mexico and Guatemala, the Maori in Australia. Farmers in South Korea and Mexico, France and Peru link together to challenge American trade restrictions on agricultural goods. A once isolated rural community in Chiapas finds not only support but the makings of a practical political alliance—the makings of power—in this linking of local identities.

This emergent universality—of linked localities and networked nodes—has its characteristic forms of warfare as well. Modernity once appeared as the age of total war, in which vast armies and, behind them, mobilized societies faced each other armed with weapons of mass destruction, culminating in the mutually assured destruction of the age of atomic warfare. Yet as the twentieth century wore on, it became possible to look back and see another form of warfare coming to the fore. The age of total war would also be the age of partisan warfare, the age of the guerrilla.

The Spanish guerrillas who met Napoleon's invasion, the maquis in Vichy France, the guerrilla wars of Algeria, Cuba, and Vietnam, present another form of warfare belonging to the age. In this form, warfare is local and particular. The guerrilla strikes and withdraws. Guerrillas may acknowledge no central authority, they can function as bands bound to one another by a common aim or loyalty, cooperating, perhaps, but able to respond to local conditions and opportunities, protected by their ignorance of one another. When Che Guevara referred to the guerrilla as "the Jesuit of war," Carl Schmitt took him to refer to the guerrilla's absolute commitment. Guevara might also have referred to the guerrilla's capacity for discrimination, for nice distinctions, for strategies crafted to a particular end and aim. War took on some of the attributes of the nineteenth-century anarchists' system of cells: small, intensely local and particular, knowing little of other cells, but bound by ideology and, through communication, in an international network. These forms of warfare, particular, adaptable, responsive, did not remain confined to resistance and rebellion. We can see them in two features of the war in Iraq and Afghanistan: precision bombing and the "Army of One."

If the guerrilla is the Jesuit of war, then one might all too aptly call precision bombing jesuitical. Precision bombing is the work of the active mind: trained and technical. It makes fine distinctions—between the government office and the grocery, the chemist and the chemical plant—and enables onlookers, linked to the war by a network of command control and communication, to see the war as selection rather than destruction and to pretend that it touches only the dangerous and the guilty, not the innocent. Careful targeting does not, however, spare the random passerby, the cleaning lady at work in the closed offices, the janitor taking out the trash, the deliverymen on their morning rounds. Careful targeting may spare the workers at the electrical plant, but collateral damage will include homes and hospitals as well as military operations.

"An Army of One" was the United States Army's recruiting slogan as the war in Iraq began. The slogan might have been thought to be no more than a rhetorical strategy to cast an aura of individuality over the determined mass discipline of the military enterprise. The campaign was accompanied, however, by research that aimed to alter the relation of the soldier to the force. Each soldier would be dressed in lightweight gear enabling that soldier to operate independently and yet remain part of the force. The soldier's vital signs would be monitored so that the force would know whether the soldier was alive, dead, or wounded. The soldier's location would be monitored so that the soldier could be deployed more effectively—more locally—with an eye to particular conditions. The soldier would be able to communicate with the force, transmitting more-precise information. The soldier would be linked to the force in a vast network of control and surveillance. The soldier would be able to operate more individually, and less independently. In a very practical sense, the soldier would operate as an army of one, for each soldier would be a link to the army as a whole, and bring that army with him.

Conflict no longer emerges on the periphery, at the boundaries, aiming to take the center. Conflict may flare at any point, flaming from some knot of local conflict, spreading through its links. The conflict in Palestine spreads to Paris, from Ramallah to the *banlieues d'Islam* (the communities of Arab immigrants in France); the conflict in Kosovo is mediated by Saudi charities and NATO peacekeeping forces. At each site of conflict, local and global issues are joined. There is no boundary to defend, no heartland that can be sheltered from a conflict, no zone of security that can be established. Security can no longer be left to the border guards, to the army. Security becomes an attribute of daily life. Where danger is decentralized, defense must be decentralized as well. Each state, each county, each town, each local police and fire station, each citizen is mobilized. Athens must become Sparta.

Ironically, this state of constant readiness, of a mobilized society, might suit the Last Man all too well. Local conflicts can be fought with smaller forces. Most citizens can remain at home, following the war, if they choose, on the television or computer screen, meeting the conflict on their tax forms and in the voting booth, or as they pass through yet another screening device, or find themselves, yet again, under surveillance. They are in the midst of war, but war does not touch them. They may be, by some mischance, victims of a terrorist strike, but terrorists will strike only a few. Most citizens can watch the coverage of the war, or not, as they choose. For them, war may be a matter of grave reflection, of politics, or it may be a matter of passing interest, a passage on the news, a source of evening entertainment. They will not be likely to face the decision to kill. They will not have to decide for themselves the merits of the proposition that modernity disputed: *dulce et decorum est, pro patria mori.*

War seemed to Carl Schmitt, and still seems to some of the students of Leo Strauss, to be the activity which would restore seriousness to life. Leon Kass wrote after 9/11, "In numerous if subtle ways, one feels a palpable increase in America's moral seriousness." That moral seriousness was not a matter of reflection. Instead, "A fresh breeze of sensible moral judgment, clearing away the fog of unthinking and easy-going relativism, has enabled us to see evil for what it is." War restored a clarity that thought had undermined. War would restore virtue as well. Without war, heroism and courage, valor and sacrifice are lost. In war, men choose the loyalties that they had received thoughtlessly, through birth or kinship. In war, men choose to die; in peace, death is forced upon them. In war, men die willingly for one another, for their comrades, their country, their faith.

War rescues men from the hazards of civilization. War forces men to consider their loyalties and their allegiance: war makes men thoughtful. War forces men to make decisions peace would forestall: war makes men decisive. War separates men from women, and restores to them the virtues they had in another age: war makes men manly. War places greatness within the reach of ordinary men. *Dulce et decorum est, pro patria mori.*

This is the romance of war. Consider it again. In war, death is forced upon many men: the willing and the unwilling, the volunteer and the draftee, the one who gives his life for his country and the deserter scurrying backwards as the shell hits. In war, one soldier gives his life for his country's freedom, as across the field, in another foxhole, another trench, another quadrant, another soldier dies to see that country conquered and the extent of his own empire extended. In war, one gives his life for the Aryan race, another that all men can live as equals. One gives his life for King and Country, another for the Rights of Man. In war, men kill other soldiers, other men, women, children, the aged and the infirm, the weak with the strong. The time is long past when people could believe that war touched only soldiers. Precision bombing will not bring it back. In war, men kill: for one another, for their comrades, for their country, for their faith. Which of these is honored in that killing? War faces the dishonored, the ordinary, the weak, and the timid with the need for acts of nobility and sacrifice. They may rise to meet that need. War faces the honorable with the necessity of dishonorable actions, confronts the noble with the need to commit small crimes and cruelties. They are obliged to meet those needs as well. I have never heard the lament for the loss of war from men who fought it. They would not tell the old familiar story of *dulce et decorum est, pro patria mori.*

Nor, I think, would they subscribe to the view that war removes men from the hazards of civilization. If we are to fear that civilization will make men sheep, too ready to obey commands, war ought not to reassure us. If we are to fear the emergence of mass culture, we ought to look with some anxiety on military discipline, the films of John Wayne, and the careers of Ronald Reagan. If we are to fear the aesthetization of life, that life will become a matter of style rather than substance, then we should turn that anxiety to the taste for military uniform and the films of Leni Riefenstahl and Steven Spielberg. If we are to fear a culture of entertainment, we should consider what is said in the broadcasts of embedded journalists and the television news.

These romantic theorists of war thought the threat of death would force reflection on the unwilling. The confrontation with an enemy would remind us of what we valued, of the essential qualities that might define us. Life would no longer be a middle-class existence of great comforts and small choices, security and entertainment. As the shape of the world has changed, and power has taken on the form not of a uniform field but of an interrupted and irregular network, the hazards of a world made one seem to have changed. What war offers has changed with it. If wars are fought by volunteers, then war becomes a choice, a choice of occupation, impelled by economics and identity, not by an immediate confrontation with an enemy. If war is—for those who do not fight it—something that one may escape by changing the channel, or turning the page, war is another choice of entertainment.

The wars of the present moment are, for those of us in the United States, wars of the Last Man. We watch if we choose; or we change the channel. We needn't watch much, even if we leave

the news on. There are no flag-draped coffins, for photojournal-
ists are forbidden to photograph the bodies returning to Dover
Air Base from Afghanistan and Iraq. There is no mourning of the
dead. There are no photos of soldiers returning home missing a
limb or two. There is, very occasionally, news coverage showing
Iraqi casualties. I have never seen these alien casualties counted
in the American press. There are flags on cars, and in elaborate
patriotic ceremonies at high schools and halftimes. The students
I teach, though they are of military age, have no thoughts of
going to war. In the wars of the Last Man, sacrifice and heroism
are reserved to the reservists, who went to war so they could go
to college. They don't come to the Ivy League. In the wars of the
Last Man, the enemy is bombed, the capital falls, the leader is captured, on camera. Regime change takes weeks of bombing in
Afghanistan and Iraq, tanks and Humvees, battles, ambushes, in-
surrection. In those places there are mines and missiles and the
sound of gunfire. The only helicopters we hear are reporting on
rush-hour traffic. The war is easy, the war is comfortable. Yet the
war is made by people in the grip of fear.

Soccer moms on the radio, policy makers on television tell us
that nothing is the same since 9/11. We live in fear, they say.
They saw the twin towers of the World Trade Center burning,
and though they were too far to smell the smoke, though they
knew no one lost in the disaster, though they live and work and
shop in the suburbs, they are afraid. They accept, happily, the

searches at airports, the metal detectors in public buildings, the provisions permitting searches without a warrant. They would, perhaps, accept much more. They believe that they are in danger, and that these tools, practices, and provisions stand between them and danger.

Sheldon Wolin saw the shape of this order coming into being. We of the West, he wrote, were becoming, paradoxically, more fearful as we became ever more heavily armed. "Let me advance a highly tentative observation," he wrote in 1962. "The *intensity* of violence in certain instances has increased, aside from the new scientific weapons of destruction, while our capacity for enduring violence has diminished." Forty years later, we can confirm this tentative assessment. We command weapons at all levels of destructiveness. We have refined our capacity to inflict violence, from weapons of mass destruction to instruments for crowd control. We command weapons of varied intensity and extreme precision. We employ them at home and abroad, with little notice. Iraq was bombed sporadically for more than ten years, with each run meriting no more than a brief mention in the press. We have used force—apart from the war in Vietnam—in Grenada, Panama, Bosnia, and Somalia. Our capacity for enduring violence has more than diminished, it has gone below zero. We are afraid, and we deploy considerable violence in consequence, at the mere prospect of an imminent threat. This has produced, as Wolin forecast, an acceleration in the development of the violence we fear: "One paradoxical result of these protective devices has been a magnification of the amount of force or violence needed for successful illegal activity." Whether it is crime at home or insurgency abroad, we have raised the bar.

There is another irony in the transformation of reckless Athens into a comfort-loving Sparta, one that Xenophon's dialogue makes all too clear. The tyrant's life, the tyrant tells us, is made unendurable by fear. "Tyrants believe they see enemies not only in front of them, but on every side." Yet they cannot let tyranny go. The measures they have taken to protect themselves have made that impossible. "For how would some tyrant ever be able to repay in full the money of those he has dispossessed, or suffer in turn the chains he has loaded on them, or how supply in requital enough lives to die for those he has put to death?" The measures the tyrant has had to take for his own security have put him in danger, body and soul. In assuming the tyranny, he has betrayed himself.

Once, long ago now, an American president told the people, "The only thing we have to fear is fear itself." There was much to fear then. The farms of the West, the stocks and bonds of the East dissolved into dust. Many were in poverty. Many were angry. Across the Pacific, the Japanese were assembling a great fleet. Across the Atlantic, in England as well as in Germany, fascism was rising and the nation was armed. There was reason for fear. Fear had to be set aside. Americans fed the poor, restored the economy, readied their forces. They were unafraid.

There is less to fear now, but the fear is greater. Those who have never heard a gunshot, who live far from the centers of power, fear a terrorist attack. They believe they see enemies on every side. The measures they take to protect themselves place their lives, their liberties, and their honor in danger.

10 *Conservatism Abandoned*

Straussians are conservative. Why they are conservative remains something of a mystery. Strauss's work on Plato or Xenophon or other figures in the canon does not lead inevitably to conservatism. That Strauss himself was a conservative should matter very little. Hegel recommended monarchy and is still read and admired in liberal democracies. Feminists make use of Nietzsche and Rousseau. Republicans admire the Southern Agrarians. Teachers do not clone, they teach. Great teachers will produce students very unlike themselves. As Nietzsche wrote,

> All who climb on their own way
> Carry my image, too, into the breaking day.

Once upon a time, I am told, there were liberal and left Straussians. That has changed. Those species have become extinct, dying out in the aftermath of the cosmic events of the late sixties. As Strauss's students became outnumbered by his disciples, politics—the politics of the moment—overcame philosophy. Strauss's followers have been exclusively conservative in my time. They grow less conservative every day.

The American conservatism that embraced Strauss had a clear commitment to certain simple tenets. Conservatives reverenced custom and tradition. They believed that with wealth and power came responsibility. They resisted change. They distrusted abstract principles, grand theories, utopian projects. They prided themselves on their regard for education and the arts. Above all, they advocated a small government. This disposition, and the political positions that expressed it, have a long and honorable history. In our time, American conservatism has departed from the cautious principles of this tradition.

American conservatives of an earlier era followed the British statesman and theorist Edmund Burke in his respect for custom and the wisdom embedded in practices long established. Burke had been sorry to see the British empire let the American colonies go. The author of a famous "Speech on Reconciliation with the Colonies" spoke presciently of America's future strength and enduring ties to Britain. America and Britain, Burke argued, were held together by "ties which, though light as air, are strong as links of iron." They shared common names and common blood, but above all, they shared a common constitution, common history, and common customs. Time, experience, and habit had made them alike.

Custom was not mere accident for Burke, or the residue of history. Custom was the repository of knowledge greater than the narrow compass of one man's life, acquired over generations. Burke praised prejudice, by which he meant habits of mind and taste, that moved the people of a place to do things in a particular way. Prejudice, as later philosophers would agree, was not mere irrationality; rather, it expressed the dispositions, inclinations, and preferences of a community. Communities shaped themselves in time, responding to the dictates of reason, of course, but also to the demands of their particular conditions. Their dispositions and inclinations went beyond the reasonable because they responded to conditions beyond the reach of individual reason. They expressed the history and character of the community, they preserved that history and a given set of relations.

We should defer to such things, conservatives argued, because the knowledge of generations is greater than our own, and because we wish to preserve our links to those who came before us. Abstract reasoning and utopian projects were dangerously prone to error. Their failures produced chaos and disruption. Their success, however great, severed links to the past and destroyed the distinctive character of a community created in the slow movement of time. Conservatives of this cast, like Edmund Burke, valued custom and practice, revered memory, and honored the distinctive character of an established community sharing a common life.

This conservative tradition has taken several forms in America. Not all have been regarded always and everywhere as conservative, but all have reflected Burke's conservative sensibility. Appropriately, the regard for tradition has been strongest in those places where a common life was formed by generation after generation living (often farming) in a single place. The varied traditions of New England and the South found common ground in a sense of the abiding presence of the past. These conservatives have sought to preserve a common life. The Southern Agrarians, though they varied in their attitudes to politics and religion, met in their love of the land and in their belief that the practice of farming drew those who lived on the land into a more intimate relation with it. They would live much as their ancestors did. Though they might use different tools than those who farmed before them, they would know the same rhythms of life, be bound to the same seasons, and look for the same changes in weather. They were bound with the land, those who lived upon it, and with those who had lived there before them. The rhythms of nature in planting and harvesting, in the busy and the fallow months, gave lives an order that echoed across generations.

Farming kept the bonds between generations. Farming kept the bonds between classes as well. Whether they were rich or poor, whether they farmed much land or little, these farmers knew the same concerns. They wanted the rains to begin or end, they were inclined to support the same economic policies. Owner or laborer, they saw the same crops grow and smelled the same scents from the same earth. In this view, the senses and a life built around the land held people together, overcoming differences of wealth and power as well as differences made by the passage of time.

These earlier conservatives, wishing to preserve a community and carry history forward, feared those things that would break the bonds holding a community together. They were not all agrarians, though all—instructed less by Marx and Marxism than by the industrial conflicts of the nineteenth century—recognized the hazards industrial life posed to the community. Like British Prime Minister Benjamin Disraeli, whose novel *Sybil; or, the Two Nations* portrayed a society torn apart by the distance between rich and poor, they believed in the duties of privilege. In *Sybil* and the "Young England" movement, Disraeli crafted a vision that a contemporary sensibility might call compassionate conservatism, in which privilege was linked to duties of care. Like Disraeli, these American conservatives looked to myth to recall the privileged to their duties, and to console the unfortunate. Not all could be wealthy, not all could be well born, well educated, or well bred. The wealthy and privileged must be taught to ease the lot of the poor, advance the gifted and hardworking, and protect the vulnerable. The poor, the weak, the unfortunate should look to the privileged for protection and learn to find honor in their humble condition. This strand of conservatism cultivated what another, quite different, politics would call an ethic of care. American philanthropy owes much to it. This was not, however, simply a sense of noblesse oblige allied to Puritan policy making. Insofar as it followed Disraeli, it also recognized the power of the imagination to transform experience, and to shape political desire. This was a conservatism of the imagination, crafting a vision that made hierarchy palatable, even inviting.

All of these required more than civility. The communities that conservatives longed to maintain were held together by deep personal bonds. There were duties and obligations of loyalty, fidelity, care, and protection. People were expected to fulfill those duties and to do so without self-congratulation or complaint. Common bonds required more than common courtesy. Those who lived in a place generation after generation learned that community required attention to people's pride as well as their welfare. Perhaps for this reason, traditional conservatives prided themselves on manners: on responses that were not merely civil but gracious, on conduct that went beyond decency to generosity. Though bearing and manner were often thought to be legacies of a lost aristocratic order, they served democracy well. The civil citizen could have the bearing and the grace of an aristocrat, as long as the citizen extended that civility to the others.

This strand of conservatism was bound to another that valued the beautiful, the elegant, the difficult, the cultured. Conservatives remain fond of Alexis de Tocqueville's nostalgia for the lost world of the aristocracy. They have retained Burke's affection for the forms of beauty he called sublime. They believe that democracy is careless with the beautiful, frustrated by the difficult, and prone to produce a world of utility rather than elegance. They set themselves the task of preserving the arts that democracy endangers. Allied to these has been the recognition that cultured tastes require cultivation. Arts required patrons with the leisure to acquire knowledge and the money to employ it. Arts required artists. Artists required time and training, and enough patronage to provide a livelihood. Conservatism also cultivated the crafts and craftsmen that made life elegant and beautiful: gardeners, architects, horse breeders, furniture makers. These forms of patronage were not only cultivated by but characteristic of traditional American conservatism.

For some American conservatives, love of one's surroundings and a fear of loss led to other efforts at preservation. Conservation has not been solely the preserve of liberals in America. Conservatives were led to it by the fundamentally *conservative* desire to preserve the old and the beautiful. In doing so, one might preserve links to one's memory and history, to one's own childhood and the experiences of one's ancestors. A conservatism that valued life in a place would value that place as well. Conservatives allied themselves to efforts at historic preservation and attempts at preserving elements of an architectural heritage.

American conservatives had, appropriately, practical as well as intellectual links to their English forebears. Like the English, Americans of wealth and power prided themselves on having a country life: hunting, fishing, riding. They learned to love the land as a place for living. They allied with other, perhaps more American conservatives, whose passion was for the land itself. The wild lands, the untouched places, had their own beauty. Conservative affection for the land and awe before the sublime led many into the conservation movement.

In America, the conservative tradition was, as this history suggests, largely an English tradition. It had other English political ancestors. The ideas of the country party republicans grew better in American than they had in English soil. They held that, in the American formulation, "that government is best that governs least." They resisted the growth of the state. A small state furnished at least two benefits to the citizens: it cost them less and it intruded less on their lives.

American conservatives particularly resisted the expansion of the federal government. The conservative tradition that distrusted the state extends from the Founding to the present. Like other aspects of American conservatism, it has, at certain moments, crossed the boundary dividing left and right to unite the nation. Perhaps the distrust of central authority recalls those revolutionaries who rebelled against the central authority in Britain. Perhaps, as Louis Hartz thought, it is the legacy of that moment in English history that shaped the American colonies and made them different from the motherland. Perhaps it was the memory of settling a frontier, when the state was far away and the settlers were thrown back on their own devices, their own strength. Whatever its origins, distrust of the state has remained strong in America. Americans recognized the need for power "to provide for the common defense and promote the general welfare," but they also recognized that federal power could be turned against the states and the people. They fenced it in, confined it by law and custom, disciplined its exercise. They took powers other nations had concentrated in the center and spread them out to the states, to counties, to townships, and to the people.

The distrust of strong government led to the clearest tenets of the conservative political program in America. Conservatives might differ on the value of myth or memory, the reverence given to ancestry or effort, the importance of education. They might differ on the virtues of large corporations. Southern Agrarians and those who longed for the intimate communities of the past tended to distrust the view that what was good for General Motors was good for America. Libertarians and the Christian right differed on the governance of morals. All tended, however, to number frugality among the virtues. Conservatives united in the desire for a smaller government and on the belief that taxes should—if they existed at all—be very low. Some, who grew stronger in the Reagan era, held that powers now held by the federal government should return to the states. All united in condemning the extravagances of deficit spending.

Conservatism in all its American forms was characterized by a profound respect for limits. American conservatives advocated limited government. That limited government should, more-over, hold itself firmly within other limits. Governments should have limited ambitions and limited budgets. They should op-pose grandiose plans for social transformation. Fiscal conser-vatism was a good in its own right, and an aid to keeping ambi-tious projects within bounds. Limited spending maintained private and public prosperity. Limits on government ambition, on plans and projects, would tend to keep things as they were. Keeping things as they were kept people as their ancestors had been. Respect for limits held a people to tradition, and bound them with their forebears.

Governments, conservatives thought, should work not only within the limits of the law but within the limits of custom and precedent. People should hold fast to custom and tradition, lim-iting change. They should discipline and constrain their own be-havior, holding their own conduct within moral, ethical, and even aesthetic limits. Conservatives praised the cultivation of moral virtues and ethical discipline. They praised the dignified, disciplined, and elegant bearing of those who kept their emo-tions and their conduct within bounds. They preferred restraint in dress and decoration as well. Political conservatism favored aesthetic conservatism. There were, of course, differences and tensions among varieties of American conservatives. Some con-servatives favored the governance of public morals, others ar-gued for limiting government's intrusions into the private realm. Though they differed in their philosophies and tactics, even these diverse and often opposed conservatisms concurred in their regard for limits. Respect for limits would maintain private virtue and public order.

In the latter part of the twentieth century, American conservatism flourished. Conservatives devoted time and thought to their ideas, and worked to see them spread throughout the culture. These academic conservatives were cranky: at odds with their colleagues of the left and center, and often with each other. Strauss and Voegelin, Hayek, Rothbard, and Kendall had allies in more popular writers and public intellectuals. The right, once the province of obscure groups obscurely at odds with the prejudices, preferences, and passions of Americans, found a receptive audience. Reagan's nostalgic picture of a vanished America returned with the phrase "It's morning in America." Americans read Miss Manners and William Bennett. Parents argued for the restoration of standards of dress and conduct in schools. A philosophy of limits found expression in term limits, limits on welfare spending and time on welfare, limits on government intervention and government spending. Budget deficits were condemned as morally corrupt and politically dangerous. Balancing the budget became a standard of public, if not private, rectitude.

All this changed as the twentieth century ended. American conservatism embraced big government with a vengeance. Conservatives had once resisted the enlargement of the state; now they argued for the extension of its powers. The creation of the Department of Homeland Security expanded the size of the federal government dramatically. The effective powers of the federal government increased with it. Existing arms of the federal government, notably the Justice Department, used the powers they had more vigorously, and claimed other powers not previously granted. As the government grew, citizens felt its weight more heavily. Anyone who took a plane or passed through a metal detector at some obscure county office came under its gaze. Some (but only some) had to register. Some (but only some) who wished to follow the path of my great-grandparents and become citizens found that option foreclosed, found themselves or their husbands and brothers imprisoned or deported without a hearing. The deficit grew.

The conservatives of the past knew well: nothing expands a government like a war. In the United States, wars have had the additional effect of disproportionately expanding the powers of the federal government. Making war is the task of the federal government. Use of the war-making power strengthens and expands it. Conservatives, still nominally wedded to the idea of a small and frugal government, caviled at the cost of Bush's "compassionate conservatism" but accepted without a murmur the burgeoning expenses of the Iraq war. Behind the vast expense of that war, others waited in the wings, as President Bush and the Defense Department forecast an endless war against terror.

There were other, perhaps more profound, departures from a conservative ethos. Trickle-down economics was accepted without a murmur. Conservatives who had once spoken of a duty to the less fortunate now contented themselves with the prospect of the poor waiting to cadge the leftovers from the overflowing tables of the prosperous. Where conservatives once reminded each other of the necessity of providing for employees and neighbors in need, they now simply locked themselves into gated communities. America came to resemble Disraeli's "two nations, between whom there is no intercourse and no sympathy; who are as ignorant of each other's habits, thoughts and feelings as if they were dwellers in different zones, or inhabitants of different planets, who are formed by a different breeding, are fed by a different food, are ordered by different manners and are not governed by the same laws."

In such a country, common myths and common memory divide as experience divides, and civility declines. The old regard for manners, for courtesy, gave way with the ascent of Rush Limbaugh to a more contentious and divisive politics. Practices once confined to talk radio became common in the more refined circles of the *National Review* and the *Weekly Standard*. Political journalism, which once tried for gravitas, adopted the sardonic style of adolescent boys. Distinguished jurists, once paragons of propriety, abandoned their concern with conduct and appearances. Supreme Court Justice Antonin Scalia refused to recuse himself from cases involving his friend and fellow duck hunter Vice President Richard Cheney, arguing, with a disdain for the conventions that would have made a nihilist proud, that only he could determine the standard by which he was to be judged.

Other virtues fell out of the canon. William Bennett dropped frugality from *The Book of Virtues*. An older and more elegant restraint in dress and manner fell out of use among these new conservatives.

Appeals to history and memory, the fear of losing old virtues, of failing to keep faith with the principles of an honored ancestry, came to seem curious and antiquated. In their place were the very appeals to universal, abstract principles, the very utopian projects that conservatives once disdained. Conservatives had once called for limits and restraint; now there were calls to daring and adventurism. Conservatives had once stood steadfastly for the Constitution and community, for loyalties born of experience and strengthened in a common life. Now there were global projects, and crusades.

Nowhere was the shift more apparent than among the Straussians active in Washington. The gulf between rich and poor had expanded without a murmur from the ostensible conservatives of the intellectual class. The repeal of those taxes most burdensome to the very wealthy, combined with the decline in jobs and the removal of aspects of the social welfare system, made America two nations. In one nation, wealth bred wealth, and wealth passed from one generation to the next. In the other, people found themselves drawing their families more deeply into debt. In one nation, executives, forgetting their duties to stockholders and workers, paid themselves lavishly without regard for performance. They forgot the boundaries separating private enjoyment from public goods and spent company funds on lavish parties of astonishing vulgarity. The sense of limits that conservatives had once used to regulate private conduct and the conduct of business was abandoned.

The traditional concern for conservation had once united West and East in a common affection for the land. Conservation had crossed the boundaries of party and partisanship, uniting hunters and vegans, Democrats and Republicans. Even Teddy Roosevelt's enthusiasm for unspoiled places could not hold. The Arctic was opened for drilling, public lands were opened to exploitation. The old conservative regard for beauty and the sublime fell before the new conservative enthusiasm for profit. The old conservative conception of a common heritage, a common patrimony, fell by the wayside. "Homeland," which once recalled a farmhouse in a hometown, or the grandeur of the Rockies and the broad stretches of the western plains, came to modify "security."

As the partisans of the Project for a New American Century had argued, their vision of America's role required more: more executive-branch energy and more federal action, more military funding, more arms, more money. They had made no bones about the need for larger budgets. Frugality was for the timid. The robust internationalism of Teddy Roosevelt's latter-day disciples required an open hand. Like apathy and indifference, parsimony would lead to the collapse of the international order. "Excessive budget cuts" had led to declining military strength. Where conservatives had once condemned spendthrifts, urged economic caution, and praised the balanced budget, Bill Kristol and Robert Kagan spurred the government to sustain the higher levels of military spending necessary to sustain their vision of expansive—we might say expensive—internationalism.

As the doctrine gave way to the practice of preemption, and strategic planning gave way to making war, other conservative virtues were abandoned. Respect for the ancient tenets of just-war theory and the norms of international order were set aside. The lawful, cautious, and prudent gave way to the impulsive and opportunistic. The United States was to seize the moment: the moment of its hegemony impelled by the moment of fearful reaction. The Project for a New American Century conceived an ambitious plan. The second George Bush made it a utopian crusade, declaring, "We will rid the world of evil-doers" in "this crusade, this war on terrorism." The United States was in Iraq and in Afghanistan in pursuit not only of terrorists but of a new world order, conceived in accordance with abstract principles of right and rights. Straussian intellectuals and Straussian publications hailed that course in terms alien to the conservative disposition.

A war-making presidency—any war-making presidency—has elements of presidential autocracy about it. When Congress defers, granting to the president the free exercise of those powers without caution, counsel, or question, the powers grow greater.

Irving Kristol, the "godfather of neoconservatism" (and the father of William Kristol), has given neoconservatism an autobiography. In his portrait we can see the main features of the power that has come to rule in our time. Above all, Kristol declares, neoconservatism is active, seizing the full force of sovereignty. The powers an older conservatism had questioned and declined are taken up by neoconservatives, as one might wield a weapon or a powerful tool. Restraint in the exercise of power is a virtue no longer.

Kristol confirms that neoconservatism is a radical departure from traditional American conservatism. Neoconservatives, Kristol tells us, "politely overlook" older conservative politicians—Coolidge, Hoover, Eisenhower, and Goldwater. They overlook older conservative theorists, the settled opinions, habits, and tastes of an older and more venerable world. They have lost—or perhaps rejected—a long history of conservatism in America and England, a tradition that gave America a memory of ancestry, that preserved a history. They are not preservers; they are (as they will tell you) revolutionaries.

Irving Kristol presents neoconservatism as altogether American: an optimistic ideology born of a new world. Neoconservatism is, he declares, "distinctly American": optimistic, cheerful, robust. "There is nothing like neoconservatism in Europe, and most Europeans are highly skeptical of its legitimacy." The rejection of neoconservativism in Europe, Kristol contends, is a consequence of its American character. Kristol's account of the substance of neoconservatism shows a political movement deeply indebted to the European right.

Neoconservative foreign policy begins, for Kristol, with Thucydides, as Leo Strauss and Donald Kagan taught him. Read the theses that Kristol marks as central to American neoconservatism: patriotism, zealously cultivated; a fear of world government and the international institutions that might lead to it; and finally, and most revealingly, the ability "to distinguish friends from enemies." These tenets belong not to Thucydides, for whom world government meant, if it meant anything, the ambitions of Darius, but to a much more recent European, Carl Schmitt. It is Schmitt, not Thucydides, who regards the distinction between friend and enemy as the foundation of politics, and Schmitt who, echoed by Strauss and Kojève, warned of the dangers of world government and international institutions.

Europeans may indeed be skeptical of American neoconservatism, but their skepticism comes not because they have seen nothing like it but because they knew its progenitors too well. Neoconservatives want a strong state, and a state that will put its strength to use, a situation all too familiar to Europe. Neoconservatives would have that state ally itself with—and empower—corporations, with tax cuts targeted to stimulate the economy. Neoconservatives reject the vulgarity of mass culture. They deplore the decadence of artists and intellectuals. They, though not always religious themselves, ally themselves with religion and religious crusades. They encourage family values and the praise of older forms of family life, where women occupy themselves with children, cooking, and the church, and men take on the burdens of manliness. They see in war and the preparation for war the restoration of private virtue and public spirit. They delight in the profusion of flags: flags on cars, flags on houses, flags worn in lapels. Above all, Irving Kristol writes, neoconservatism calls for a revival of patriotism, a strong military, and an expansionist foreign policy.

In its principles, as its principals lay them out, neoconservatism is not the *res Americana*, the American thing, but a rather recent European import. Consider again the program set forth by the neoconservatives. They want "a strong state" with a strong leader. They speak favorably of authoritarian leaders and argue that America would profit from a more authoritarian democracy. They favor the expansion of executive power. They want that strong state to have an expansive and expansionist foreign policy—to, as they say, "make trouble" in the world. They hope—they plan—to establish a new world order to rival Rome. The new world order will, they recognize, be established not with the consent of the governed but through force. Military power is essential to a robust foreign policy, to forging the *Pax Americana*. Military power is praised. The neoconservative economic program speaks to the concerns of small businesses, small property owners, and working people. The appeals to ordinary people are matched by benefits given to the extraordinary: the wealthiest individuals and corporations. They combine populist rhetoric with a corporatist strategy. They encourage citizens to "police" their neighbors and to inform the government of suspicious activities. They favor the establishment of stronger police powers and more extensive intelligence at home, with fewer constraints and greater powers of surveillance.

What caused Straussian neoconservatives to abandon an older Anglo-American conservatism for this? Perhaps it was the hubris bred by too much power obtained too quickly. Perhaps, like Jefferson faced with the offer of Louisiana, they believed that opportunity should overcome restraint. Perhaps a conservatism bred in the American context to be primarily preoccupied with domestic matters found itself unmoored when considering foreign policy. Perhaps fear bred fear until the once conservative could no longer distinguish friend and enemy in the fog of an unending war. Perhaps it was the allure of empire.

11   *The Sicilian Expedition*

In the years after World War II, America found itself not only "great among the nations," as Teddy Roosevelt had hoped, but an imperial hegemon. America held death in its hand, or so Americans thought. The sole possession of nuclear weapons conferred a brief unchallenged primacy. There were those who thought that America should seize the moment of its ascendancy, suppress the communists by force of arms, and so secure the Free World. Those who read Thucydides as an admonition feared this enthusiastic imperial ambition. George Kennan was perhaps the most famous of those who held to this reading of Thucydides. America, they argued, should resist the temptation to annihilate totalitarianism at a blow. That course would plunge the world again into war, a war (like that Thucydides had experienced) with no certain outcome. Rather, America should pursue, with its allies, a policy of containment. This was the view advanced by Kennan in his famous memorandum advocating containment rather than confrontation. Kennan's "Long Telegram" of 1946, later published in *Foreign Affairs* as "The Sources of Soviet Conduct," laid out the policy that triumphed in American foreign policy after the Second World War, the policy that preserved peace between antagonists armed with nuclear weapons.

Albert Wohlstetter eroded this reading of Thucydides in his classes at the University of Chicago on nuclear war. Wohlstetter made his reputation by advocating limited use of nuclear weapons. If we could not employ weapons that would result in annihilation, we might consider the use of smaller weapons for tactical purposes.

By the late 1970s Wohlstetter was an old man with a white beard and erratic teaching habits. Unlike most people at Chicago, Wohlstetter seemed largely unconcerned with teaching or writing or the questions that belonged to the life of the mind. He seemed to cancel as many classes as he taught, and when he appeared he was as likely to tell anecdotes as give analyses. He taught little formulae like the three Cs (command, control, communication). He taught us to call the dire warnings about nuclear annihilation "pacific terribilism."

Wohlstetter was no Straussian, but he had a certain cadet line relation to the lineages of the Straussians who came to power. This relation was enhanced in later years, as Straussians who had joined the networks of Rand and Republican administrations recommended the writings of Wohlstetter and his wife, Roberta, to their more philosophically inclined colleagues. In earlier years, Wohlstetter had offered the Straussians an ally in the field of international relations. He marked the possibility that one might move out of the academy and acquire other forms of influence. He had taught Paul Wolfowitz.

Wolfowitz was part of a cohort who came to Strauss, and to Chicago, from Allan Bloom. That group included Catherine and Michael Zuckert, Thomas Pangle, and Abram Shulsky, who was thought—at least by the students—to be the cleverest of the cohort. Wolfowitz was not, as so many of Bloom's students were, wholly committed to political philosophy. He was as much a student of Wohlstetter as a student of Strauss, and still very much a student of Bloom.

Wolfowitz was a curious presence in Chicago in later years. We all knew his name, which was surprising in itself because he had done something normally regarded as a form of failure. He had left the academy. No one spoke of what Wolfowitz thought, or what he had written. Wolfowitz worked for the government. I presumed, because people remembered him, that he had been a good student. His leaving the academy for the government had, therefore, an element of altruism about it. He had left the academy to serve his country. The ghostly (if not *geistliche*) presence of Wolfowitz offered professors—Cropsey, Storing, Tarcov—an opportunity to acknowledge government service as an honorable profession. At Harvard or Princeton, government service occupies a place of privilege. One pursues power, and if one is fortunate, one acquires it. At Chicago, one pursued the life of the mind. There was nothing higher, there was nothing else. One might be unfortunate and fail to obtain an academic job (there was no sense that these were awarded on merit alone) and then one would need a job for food and shelter, but the only accomplishments that mattered were those of the mind. From time to time one would be told of someone who made a great deal of money, making wine or trading on the stock exchange, but these accounts were always bittersweet. Nothing could compensate for what they had lost. Where intellectual passion is so highly valued, it is necessary from time to time to remind students that there are other honorable professions. Albert Wohlstetter opened the door into one of them.

Wohlstetter belonged to another world: the world of the policy-making coasts: the world of Washington and Rand. He flew between Chicago and Washington, between Chicago and various think tanks, often forgetting to teach a class, and teaching very casually on those occasions when he did appear. Chicago students are not very forgiving of that sort of thing, and perhaps it was as a kind of recompense that Wohlstetter invited the class to a reception at his house. He didn't live, as most of the professors did, in Hyde Park, an old, integrated neighborhood of four-flats and apartments. He lived at the edge of Lincoln Park in an elegant and lavish apartment, where we drank champagne and ate strawberries. This wasn't the life of the mind. This was the life of the privileged and powerful. I don't know why Paul Wolfowitz entered it. I do know how and why Zalmay Khalilzad did.

Khalilzad is, at the time I write this, ambassador to Afghanistan. He has also served as President Bush's special envoy, on the National Security Council, as an adviser to Rumsfeld, and as "Ambassador at Large for the Free Iraqis." He has been involved in establishing the government of Hamid Karzai in Afghanistan and the return of Ahmed Chalabi to Iraq. He is a protégé of Wolfowitz, who worked with him on the war with Iraq and the occupation. Like many of those in the Bush administration, he has moved between the Rand Corporation and the U.S. government as if there were no boundary between them. When I knew him, he was an Afghani graduate student and a radical. He boasted of the demonstrations he had organized in Beirut, of the fedayin he knew and had worked with, and of his friends who regularly visited Libyan President Muammar Qaddafi. He went to pro-Palestinian meetings. His room had a poster of Nasser in tears. He and I had taken Wohlstetter's course on nuclear war together. He didn't seem, at the time, particularly interested in the course. He was, however, enthralled by Wohlstetter's party. In the elevator, in the apartment, he kept saying how much it all cost, how expensive it was, how much money Wohlstetter must have. Later, he borrowed my copy of Kojève's *Lectures on Hegel*. When he returned it, one sentence was underlined. "The bourgeois intellectual neither fights nor works." The next summer, Wohlstetter got Khalilzad a job at Rand. I don't know what happened to the poster of Nasser.

What Wohlstetter taught was not, in its substance, an exhortation to expansion. It does not seem to prefigure the bellicose imperialism of his students in the Bush administration. He endorsed the policy of containment and deterrence championed by George Kennan. One might regard this reading, and the policy that followed it, as triumphant. It has, however, been superseded among the Straussians by an enthusiasm for empire and a determination to exploit American imperial hegemony.

This is the program of the Project for a New American Century. The project's chairman is William Kristol, its executive director Gary Schmitt, both Straussians. The project is what its name promises: a design for a century (perhaps a little longer) that is to be not merely dominated by America but thoroughly American throughout. The aim is to make the world in America's image as once, in another time, the Romans sought to remake their world. The project is being advanced on several fronts: academic, popular, and bureaucratic. One of the more popular ventures is a book edited by William Kristol and Robert Kagan, *Present Dangers*. The introductory essay Kristol and Kagan furnish lays out both the past and future, the aim and the history of America as they see it.

The past of this America has at its heart a period (and a philosophy) from Roosevelt to Reagan. Roosevelt (that is, Teddy

Roosevelt) and Reagan become the boundaries of "a tradition in American foreign policy." They also represent the boundaries of Republican dominion. Roosevelt is cited many times in the Kristol-Kagan essay, and in the essays that follow. He stands for what the editors call "a robust brand of internationalism" and an "expansive vision." He is, in short, the apostle of empire.

Teddy Roosevelt was an easterner who went west, found himself in the West: president, Roughrider, Bull Moose, the "Teddy" of the Teddy Bear. He was a conservationist, trust buster, imperialist. He had the western resistance to fences. He looked to the great expanses of the West and across the Pacific. He sought to bring open spaces within American control. He was an enthusiastic proponent of the national park system that would bring the wilderness under federal control. He wanted to bring the open spaces of the Atlantic and Pacific within American control as well. In him the western projects of expansion become open and avowed imperialism.

Roosevelt declared his philosophy—which his latter-day adherents, Kristol, Kagan, and James Caesar, call "expansive internationalism"—in a speech often called "The Strenuous Life." Roosevelt's speech begins with the West, and with warlike, conquering men of the West, Lincoln and Grant, but he makes it clear that the western character is embodied in other men as well. National character is not, for Roosevelt, a racial inheritance as it was for Senator Henry Cabot Lodge. One also had to work to become American, and for Roosevelt, the opposite of work is "peace." "We do not admire the man of timid peace," Roosevelt declared. "Peace" is used throughout the speech as a synonym for "ease" and "sloth." "Work" is the word used for war and empire building. Effort is "victorious effort." There is another word for the sort of striving, the constant strenuous effort at self-improvement that Roosevelt described. That word is *jihad*.

The Arabic word conveys the same sense of struggle. That struggle will be individual: a discipline, a regimen of self-government and self-improvement, a submission to duty and a striving after greatness. The struggle may be a political one: the struggle of a nation or a people to improve themselves, or against their enemies in war. In jihad, as in Roosevelt's understanding of "the strenuous life," the individual and national struggles are joined. That is not the only point of resemblance.

In Roosevelt's jihad, as in that of Osama bin Laden, there are clear differences in the work of men and women. Men fought, women bred. Roosevelt looked for "stern men with empire in their brains" and women who would be the "mothers of many healthy children." Imperialism is "manly." Empire is a matter of "manliness." We must not lose to a "stronger, manlier power." Kristol and Kagan are not prepared (at least not in *Present Dangers*) to argue that while men make war, women should make children. They have nothing to say about the present service of women in combat. They are, however, eager to subscribe to Roosevelt's fear of effeminacy, and argue in their own right that America has become "effete."

War, and the preparation for war, are the characteristic pursuits of "the strenuous life." The virtue of war, for Kristol, Kagan, and their cohort as for Roosevelt, is not that it leads to greater national security but that it leads to hardier and more virtuous citizens, a nation of men with what their colleague Carnes Lord would call "such traditionally manly qualities as competitiveness, aggression, or for that matter, the ability to command."

The object of imperial war, of "expansive internationalism," in Kristol and Kagan's tamer variation, is neither security, nor, in the usual sense, interest. Roosevelt did not pursue empire as Senators Henry Cabot Lodge or Albert Beveridge did, out of a sense of racial superiority or a desire to expand American trade. For Lodge, the principal object of American empire was business. America would project force in the Philippines in order to open markets, especially the China market. Roosevelt was far less interested in opening markets to American goods: he wanted to open the world to American government. The object is greatness, Roosevelt declared. "If we are to be a really great people we must play a great part in the world." If we were to play a great part in the world we must seek out conflict, impose American will, and silence those "who cant about liberty and the consent of the governed."

This is the project of *Present Dangers*. Kristol and Kagan, like Roosevelt, argue that security concerns should not determine where America uses its power. "In fact," they write, "the ubiquitous post–Cold War question—where is the threat?—is misconceived." The present danger is not war or the hazards of war, but that the United States will "shirk its responsibilities." It is not threats that should incite war, but opportunity. The United States enjoys a power "unmatched since Rome," and it should use that power. The United States must cultivate the "willingness to project force" and more: "the United States can set about making trouble."

The policy of preemption that impelled the invasions of Afghanistan and Iraq shows itself clearly here. We need to make trouble for others—rogue nations, rival powers, "hostile and potentially hostile nations"—before they make trouble for us. University of Chicago professor John Mearsheimer once put himself within an inch of a student's face, shook his fist, and asked, "Does this enhance my security?" The policy of provocation and preemption advanced in *Present Dangers* and adopted by the Bush administration got a hostile reception from the hard-headed realists in the field of international relations. John Mearsheimer, Steve Walt, Bruce Bueno de Mesquita, and Ken Waltz, eminent realists all, argued that this policy, apart from any moral and political defects, would not increase American national security; it would diminish it.

Security is not, however, the primary object of "making trouble." America's unrivaled power presents an unparalleled opportunity. America can not only be great among the nations, with a power "unmatched since Rome," it can impose upon the world a Pax Americana, or perhaps something stronger, something more strenuous, a Bellum Americanum, an American jihad. This struggle would involve the newly invigorated, manly citizens in a common project of "expansive internationalism." The nation would shake off the effeminacy and apathy of containment and extend itself. Kristol and Kagan recommended another policy adopted by the Bush administration, a policy they called "regime change." The United States should seek to "bring about the demise of the regimes" that might threaten the United States in the first instance, and seek in the second to remake the world. We should install, where we can, regimes that reflect American values. We should create an order where those values are not merely in the ascendant but all-encompassing. America is to find "honor and greatness in the service of liberal principles."

Present Dangers is not a conservative work. The regard for tradition, for the slow growth of custom that Burke commended, the respect for long-established practices are abandoned here. In their place is an enthusiasm for innovation, for intervention, for utopias. Nothing can wait, everything must be done now. No one need be consulted, for local custom and established preferences must fall before the rational force of liberal (yes, liberal) values. Liberal values require not the consent of the governed, but the force of arms.

Exactly what this might entail is suggested by Paul Wolfowitz's essay in *Present Dangers*, "How We Learned to Stop Worrying and Love the *Pax Americana*." The title is that most interpretable of references, one any Straussian would recognize, the quotation slightly altered. The source is the film *Dr. Strangelove, Or How I Learned to Stop Worrying and Love the Bomb*. It is apt indeed. Wolfowitz argues that the Pax Americana is to be best secured by the use of a particular type of arms: tactical nuclear weapons. If the classical interpretive schematic holds, Wolfowitz is suggesting that the Pax Americana is dependent on the willingness and ability to use nuclear weapons. This interpretation is supported by the course of Wolfowitz's career.

Wolfowitz aligned himself early in his career with those who refused to regard the nuclear weapon as weapon of last resort, much less as weapon never to be used at all. Rather than regarding nuclear weapons as weapons to be used only for deterrence, Wolfowitz and his allies argued that they should be used like other weapons. They were to be tactical as well as strategic, available not only for long-term strategies of geopolitics but for more immediate and short-term military goals. This remains, happily, the speculative boundary of what an intervention might involve.

We need not, however, look to speculative writings to discover what intervention might entail. The failure to discover weapons of mass destruction in Iraq has led the defenders of intervention to argue that the defects of the regime of Saddam Hussein were in themselves sufficient justification for war. We can therefore look to Iraq and Afghanistan as exemplary of what an intervention might accomplish. They suggest that while liberal democratic values—respect for human rights, especially the rights of women, security of one's person, the consent of the governed—provide crucial elements of the justification for intervention, they do not supply the standards governing the occupation or the installation of a successor regime. This places the initial justification in doubt.

The questions to be raised about the reasons, methods, and effects of interventionism on regimes abroad seem (perhaps with a forgivable parochialism) to fall before their effects on the American regime in the present. The project of marking out a nation's path into the future entails an understanding, and an account, of the genealogy of the authors and an account of the nation's past. The partisan sensibility—conservative, Republican—of *Present Dangers* and the Project for a New American Century comes in a tradition that extends "from Roosevelt to Reagan." This is not the Republicanism of Lincoln, nor is it the conservatism of Hamilton or Goldwater. The tradition defined by the figures of Roosevelt and Reagan is imperial. Roosevelt is the maker of empire, Reagan the engineer of another empire's fall. They mark a tradition defined by the desire for national greatness, "expansive internationalism."

The project's account of national history is equally revealing. The Founding figures briefly, the Civil War not at all. The attention to Roosevelt and the regard for his expansive internationalism is not accompanied by an account of American involvement in Panama or the Philippines. The years bracketing World War II are important. They show the error of appeasement at the outbreak of war, and American hegemony after it. The Cold War is, however, of more importance in their historical narrative. In their account, the danger presented by the Soviets in the 1970s was radically underestimated. America was saved from its errors of apathy and indifference by the Reagan-era military buildup. The fall of the Soviet Union demonstrates not the success of containment but its failure. Reagan the confrontational succeeds where the partisans of containment had failed. In this history the decade and a half since 1989 has been one of hazards and dangers: "Baghdad and Belgrade," China, North Korea, and Iran.

The history is, like all such, as interesting for what it leaves out. The fall of the Soviet Union occurs in magnificent isolation, the work of a day and a man. Ronald Reagan confronts the evil empire, he builds the "Star Wars" missile defense system, and America watches the Soviet Empire crumble. The long history of uprisings and tensions in the Warsaw Pact nations is lost. In their regard for Reagan, the authors forget Hungary in 1956, the Prague Spring of 1968, and Havel's Velvet Revolution. Pressures for opening came from within the Soviet Union as well. If the prospect of American military power was daunting, the spectacle of Western wealth was devastating. Open purses and an open press presented challenges more difficult for closed regimes to counter than those of weaponry and war. As Straussians like to remind us, wars are fought best by an energetic executive and a disciplined people.

Older histories are neglected as well. The Civil War goes unmentioned. That silence conceals the site where domestic and international politics meet. "The problem of the twentieth century," as the theorist W. E. B. Du Bois observed, "is the problem of the color line." Roosevelt straddles the narrative like a colossus, but nothing is said of Panama and the Philippines. Like Niall Ferguson, the authors construct empire as something that has come only lately to Americans. America, this history implies, is the heir of Britain. Churchill puts down the burden of empire, and Americans will shoulder it, all this in the wake of the Second World War. America had thought of empire long before.

Manifest Destiny was, for some, the creation of a great continental empire. All saw that the movement westward left dependent nations in its wake. The Cherokee, the Nez Perce, and the Navajo were neither sovereign states nor sets of individuals incorporated in the United States. They had the partial sovereignty and the dependent status of colonies. Early partisans of empire—Hamilton and Burr, Webster and Calhoun—looked longingly at Canada and Mexico. If the Monroe Doctrine did not have imperial pretensions, the architects of incursions into Mexico and Central America did. With the Spanish American War, America entered on the project of empire—but neither wholeheartedly or with a single will.

William Jennings Bryan saw American imperialism as a betrayal of American principles. If America were to repudiate the principles of its founding, Bryan prophesied, it could "not escape the punishment decreed for the violation of human rights" or avoid the penalty of self-betrayal. America is to become great among the nations not because it seeks empire but because it has rejected empire. The United States was to spread the empire of human rights by means other than war and dominion. America's glory came from standing against empire, and inspiring others to do likewise. "Because our Declaration of Independence was promulgated, others have been promulgated; because our patriots of 1776 fought for liberty, others have fought for it." One of Bryan's senatorial colleagues, reading an account of the Philippine insurgency, came to words that echoed the Declaration. You tried to hide it, he told the Senate ironically, but "the miserable Filipino got ahold of it somehow." That, Bryan said, was America's pride, a pride greater than empire. "I would not exchange the glory of this Republic for the glory of all the Empires that have risen and fallen since time began."

For another of Roosevelt's contemporaries, Senator George Hoar, the pursuit of imperial greatness was not America's willful fulfillment of divine will, it was the devil's work, "the wretched glitter and glare of empire which Satan is setting before us." From the glamour of evil, good Lord, deliver us.

Kristol and Kagan's silence on America's earlier imperial adventures enables them to present empire, the Pax Americana, as the burden of maturity rather than an adolescent adventure. The imperialism that Roosevelt embraced with such enthusiasm comes under a kinder, gentler name of "expansive internationalism." The tradition that extends from Roosevelt to Reagan appears unbroken by the Depression, and the wars in Korea and Vietnam. Here, too, this conservatism departs from its predecessors. Vietnam is not the war Americans might have won, had they been more dedicated or less divided, or had the military been given a freer hand. On the contrary, only Wolfowitz cites Vietnam. He cites it only once, and then as a dreadful mistake. Liberal and conservative meet in the condemnation of Vietnam. Some liberals have gone further, finding common ground with Straussian conservatives in the vision of a clash of civilizations and the struggle for a new world order.

This is a chiliastic struggle. Kristol and Kagan turn for their justification to Roosevelt, who saw that "the defenders of civilization must exercise their power against civilization's opponents." The defenders of liberal values stand against the forces of barbarism. They will intervene against acts that shock the moral conscience of mankind. They assume that they know without asking what shocks the moral conscience of mankind, that we will concur, and that disagreements belong to the enemies of civilization. This confidence that we know already what is unjust, what shocks mankind, enables us to know, in turn, what mankind requires: the kind of regime we should set in place. One of the neglected episodes of American history might undermine this confidence. Robert McNamara, writing in his memoir *In Retrospect*, puts forward as one of the lessons of Vietnam: "We do not have the god-given right to shape every nation in our own image, or as we choose."

There is opposition to this project of universal dominion within the conservative camp as well. In *Present Dangers* it finds a voice in William Bennett, whose assertion that "America is not interested in territorial conquest, subjugation of others, or world domination" sits uneasily with policies of regime change, and the project of an American century. Bennett has a different history to offer as well. He recalls not Hamilton's ambition but Washington's self-discipline, not the desire to have a place among the great, but Washington's advice to be wary of foreign entanglements.

Americans seem to have found the most resonant histories not in their own past but among the ancients. In the Senate and on talk radio, in the academy and on the Web, parallels from the present moment are found not in America's past but in the pasts of the Roman and Athenian empires. Laura Miller observed in the *New York Times Book Review* of March 12, 2004, that "while supporters of American foreign policy like to compare America to Athens, those with reservations turn to Rome." This is not entirely accurate. As Miller herself observers, many have read—and continue to read—Thucydides' history as an account of a "catastrophe fueled by Athenian hubris and bellicosity," and Wolfowitz's use of the phrase "Pax Americana" suggests that he welcomes the comparison to imperial Rome. Most, however, continue to regard Rome as a cautionary tale.

This is most evident in Senator Robert Byrd's sustained and articulate opposition to the expansive internationalism of the Bush administration. Byrd, a West Virginia Democrat, sees the United States as Rome poised between the Republic and the Empire, and holds fast to the Republic. He rejects the doctrine of preemption and unilateralism, seeing in them the threat of un-limited war and with it, a growing empire. In his Senate speech of March 19, 2003, he saw the United States as a Roman emperor demanding obeisance in the style of an Oriental despot. "We flaunt our superpower status with arrogance. We treat U.N. Se-curity Council members like ingrates who offend our princely dignity by lifting their heads from the carpet." The new doctrine of preemption was, he said, "understood by few and feared by many. We say that the United States has the right to turn its fire-power on any corner of the globe which might be suspect in the war on terrorism. We assert that right without the sanction of any international body. As a result, the world has become a much more dangerous place." The greatest danger, Byrd argued, was to the Constitution.

Chalmers Johnson, one of the grand figures of political sci-ence, told an interviewer at the Institute for International Stud-ies at Berkeley, "I remain enormously impressed by these brilliant speeches that Senator Robert Byrd, from West Virginia, gives week-in, week-out to an empty Senate chamber. They sound like

Cicero. They really do sound like a passionate lover of our Constitution and what it stood for. Nobody is listening to him." Johnson, the author of *Sorrows of Empire*, also saw reflected in the American situation the end of the Roman Republic. "By the end of the first century B.C., Rome had seemingly, again, 'inadvertently' acquired an empire that surrounded the entire Mediterranean Sea. They then discovered that the inescapable accompaniment, the Siamese twin of imperialism, is militarism."

The Athenian empire has, by contrast, been seized by several of the proponents of American dominion. Most famously, the distinguished classical historian Donald Kagan, father of Robert Kagan and a colleague of Allan Bloom's at Cornell, has suggested that earlier scholars and public intellectuals have read Thucydides wrong and that the Athenians failed only in not being quite imperial enough. This is the favored version of the political Straussians now.

The story of the Peloponnesian War, as the Straussians once told it, was the story of a lovely arrogant city, gone down to ruin in the pursuit of empire. Athens, the free city, in love with novelty, is led astray by an errant student of Socrates. He offers Athens the temptations of imperial power. Athens falls, and the shame of the Melian dialogues, the suffering of its prisoners in the quarry, plague, and ruin fall upon it in return. This was the story as the Straussians told it in my time. They tell it differently now.

We are on the Sicilian Expedition.

12 *Athens and Jerusalem*

Strauss's famous essay "Jerusalem and Athens: Some Preliminary Reflections" marks Athens and Jerusalem, reason and revelation, as the poles whose contending gravitational pulls defined the history of political philosophy, the two sources of wisdom, two sites of the virtuous life, always at odds, always pulling against each other. Athens was the site of the polis, the city of philosophy, the wild place of unleashed reason, the city of the agon, in love with the new, the birthplace of democracy. Jerusalem was the city of God, the city of the covenant. In this place, God spoke to the people, chose them, sent them law. Revelation supplied truths beyond the reach of reason.

For all political theorists, in America, in Europe, in the Muslim world, the scriptures of the children of Abraham are works of philosophic beauty and power. They are read and interpreted, and the interpretations are debated. Distinguished commentaries are read as well. It was in this way that I read Maimonides and ibn Tufayl with Ralph Lerner, Genesis with Leon Kass, the Koran and al Farabi with Fazlur Rahman. It was in this way that I discussed Genesis, Calvin, and Luther with Sheldon Wolin. It is in this way that I teach Genesis and al Farabi to my students. Reason and revelation are not easily reconciled, but in texts, as in human beings, they often inhabit the same space.

Athens and Jerusalem stood as orienting poles in the practice of the Straussians as well. There were the classes and debates. Classes held students (like me) from the public schools, students from Ida Crown Jewish Academy and the Catholic parochial schools of Chicago, students from Andover and Exeter. There were students who had never been to a religious service and students who had never read religious scriptures outside the church, the home, or the shul. When we read Genesis, there were students who knew the text in Hebrew, students who knew many religious commentaries on the text, and students who thought that questioning such a text was tantamount to apostasy. It used to be said that Chicago was a place where Jewish professors taught Catholic philosophy to Protestant students. For many years, it has been a place where pagan philosophy is read in the manner of the Talmud, and Catholic, Jewish, and Protestant (and now Hindu, Muslim, and Buddhist) students take tentative licks at the honeyed text.

We learned about the scriptures of the children of Abraham,

and about the religious practices of the Americans. There were long, friendly, fiercely argumentative dinners, and then there were, for other, smaller groups, the reading of the Torah, the interpretation of scripture in private. I was told, by men who went to them, that Strauss and his students met to read the scriptures on Shabbat. This is an old way of honoring the Sabbath, for both Christians and Jews. The practice of thinking through a text brings Athens to Jerusalem.

There was another reading of Athens and Jerusalem. Many of these men, professors and students, stood between Athens and Jerusalem, between the city of miscegenate democracy and the land of their fathers, between the Constitution and the covenant, between America and Israel. Some were from families who had survived the death camps, a few had escaped the camps themselves. Some of had fought in Israel in 1948 or 1967 or served in the Israeli Army in more peaceful times. Most of the Jewish students had been to Israel, many had family there. Many thought about making aliyah. The uncertainties of college students who do not know what they will do or where they will live or who they will be were given greater depth. They stood, these students, between past and present dangers, between the memory of the Holocaust and Israel's uncertain future.

Strauss's positions on Israel, on Maimonides, on Judaism, were subjects of much anecdote and debate among the Straussians, especially those Straussians who were Jews as well. One story has a pious student ask Strauss about his religious beliefs.

Strauss is said to have replied, "I am a Jew as Maimonides is a Jew." Maimonides is, of course, the great Rabbi, Rambam, but he was also a philosopher, one who loved reason, and one whose work is thought by some to bring revelation too thoroughly and comfortably within reason's compass.

The position of the Straussians is not quite that of Strauss. For these, Christian and Jew, the memory of the Holocaust is joined inseparably to the future of Israel. The history Strauss read ethically and philosophically they read politically, personally. Athens and Jerusalem moved from philosophy to history. Athens and Jerusalem became America and Israel. They are conjoined not in the relation of reason to revelation, but through history.

This echoes a view held, I think, by nearly all Americans. Working for Israel in America would make America the salvation not simply of individual Jews but of Jews as a nation. Through this alliance, America would show its commitment to democracy, to religious freedom properly understood. Through this alliance, America would show itself superior to a genocidal Europe. Europe killed Jews, America makes them at home—and defends their homeland. Europe herded Jews into ghettos and sought to annihilate them as a people. In America, Jews are free to go where they will, and the United States protects the nation of Israel. This is a source of pride for all Americans, the sign that America is not as the nations, that the New World has surpassed the Old. For some Americans it is a sign that America is joined to Israel as one chosen people to another.

America's relation to Israel offers proof that Lockean liberalism has more than liberal virtues. Israel is much that America disavows. Israel is a Jewish state, a state in which one religion has primacy. America is a secular state, in which any religion is welcome, and none may claim preeminence. Israel is a nation belonging to a particular people. America is "a teeming nation of nations." One returns to Israel. Whether one is born in the United States or comes to it, one comes new to a new world. The state of Israel must be where it is. America might be anywhere, with Americans to inhabit it. In protecting and advancing the state of Israel, Americans commit themselves, with their hands, to the idea that people may be as they choose: that democracies will take forms foreign to us, that we need not remake the world in our image. This is not liberality, for it gives to the state of Israel only that which is its due, yet it has, I think, greatness of soul. In it Americans impel their will beyond their morals, their aesthetics, even their politics, willing the presence and prosperity of commitments that are not our own. This marks a common willful commitment to democracy, a recognition of the other who is still in some sense one's own, the image of friendship. Yet in this action we forget that not all within the territory of Israel have consented to be governed.

For some, the commitment to the state of Israel goes beyond

this: in commitment to the state of Israel, America places itself in the service of God. This understanding creates another moment of unity and common purpose for a number of Straussians active in foreign policy: it enables them to make common cause with elements of Christian fundamentalism. Many Christian fundamentalists regard the protection and advancement of the state of Israel as necessary to hasten the Second Coming. The Temple must be rebuilt, the red heifer found and sacrificed. The *Left Behind* series of apocalyptic novels has spread awareness of this chiliastic anticipation beyond the fundamentalist community to millions of ordinary American readers. These novels chronicle the trials of those left behind when the faithful are assumed into heaven in a moment called "the rapture." These novels have become enormously popular. One who reads the books (or watches the videos) learns that the United Nations is the abode of the Antichrist, and that fate of the world turns on the fate of Israel.

Congressman Tom De Lay holds to this belief as well. For him, the providential significance of the joining of America and Israel is both religious and political. In a speech before the Knesset he proclaimed "the common destiny of the United States and Israel." That destiny is a providential battle, a struggle between good and evil: "These are the terms Providence has put before the United States, Israel, and the rest of the civilized world." In this moral universe, "the civilized world" faces "the Palestinian Authority" as it faced "the Nazis, fascists, and Communists before them." The civilized world has grown smaller than it was, for Europe has abandoned Israel. The Palestinians, kept behind walls, driven into ghettos, have grown strangely larger in this account, so large that "Israel must be liberated from the Palestinians." The Palestinians are not a people at all, but the avatar of the forces of darkness. Israel is "at war against evil." The Palestinians figure in De Lay's account as the providential enemy, the incarnation of the threat of evil. The providential enemy must be destroyed.

The president of the Christian Coalition, Roberta Combs, told the *New York Times*, "I heard my father all my life pray for Israel. I always had a love for Israel in my heart." The old enmity between Christian and Jew is overcome for Combs in two moments: a shared cultural conservatism and a crusade against Islam. Asked whether Christians and Jews could coexist with Muslims, she replies, "I have a real problem with that, because of my love for Christians and Jews." That love, it appears, is not quite capacious enough for Muslims. Muslims, however, may be easily erased in the new order. She says of Iraq, "Why should the official religion be Muslim? I think as Iraq becomes a democracy, there are going to be a lot of churches springing up."

The desire to see democracies prosper is profound in all Americans, and often independent of religious sentiments. This is often given as the motivating principle behind the identification of American and Israeli interests. Thus Irving Kristol writes that "the United States will always feel obliged to defend, if possible, a democratic nation against undemocratic forces." For Kristol, "that is why we feel it necessary to defend Israel today." The presentation of the alliance of the United States and Israel as an alliance of democracies has its ironies. It is often presented as a justification for undemocratic actions on the part of each party to the alliance. It is advanced as a justification for diminishing the democratic qualities in each. Among the Straussians, Israel is often admired more for its less than democratic qualities. Israel has the toughness America lacks. In these circles Israel is not merely an American ally or a cause for American concern. Israel is America's instructor. Israel has learned to discipline democracy.

Carnes Lord has argued that American statesmen should take authoritarian leaders as their models, and that the American people should develop a taste for a more authoritarian regime. For those who favor a more authoritarian America, Israel provides the model. The Israel they know is not the complex, vibrant Israel of Gershon Shafir and Yoav Peled. The Israel that they admire is not the Israel of Avi Moghrabi or Tom Segev, the investigative reporting of *Ha'Aretz* or the principled refusals of *Yesh Gvul*. Straussians in the academy admire Israel's martial virtue. They look to the Israel of Ze'ev Jabotinsky and Meir Har Zion.

For these Straussians the joining of Athens and Jerusalem is the joining of America and Israel. That fusion takes several forms: religious, martial, symbolic. One Fourth of July not long ago, a Claremont Straussian, Daniel Palm, argued that the holiday could be celebrated best by turning to Israel for the recovery of the virtues we have lost. "Americans have lost some of our political seriousness and intensity. Our survival skills as a nation grow rusty." Israel has learned that it "must keep spirit strong and training up to par." Having no inspiring figures of our own in recent memory, Americans should look for patriotism else-where: in the American past, and in Israel. "This Independence Day, remember not only our country's founding principles and leaders, but the spirited patriotism and sacrifice of Jonathan Netanyahu." Here the conflation of America and Israel is com-plete: one celebrates Israeli heroes—military heroes—on the Fourth of July.

The presumption that American interests are at one with the interests of Israel—whether for secular or religious reasons—is a cornerstone of American foreign policy. The grand strategy that Paul Wolfowitz framed in the wake of 9/11 entailed a plan, an-nounced throughout the media, for attacking not only Iraq but Syria and southern Lebanon. The United States, recognizing its own power and using it willfully, would inaugurate a new order in the Middle East. The plan was built conceptually and geo-graphically around the centrality of Israel. Israel was democratic, hence protecting Israel was protecting democracy, however un-democratic the actions required, however undemocratic the re-gional consequences. States surrounding Israel, states which pre-sented a threat to Israel, would be attacked . . . preemptively. This strategy could be understood as advancing American inter-ests and security only if one saw those as identical to the interests and security of the state of Israel.

The conflation of the interests of America and Israel has had effects on American governmental practices as well as on American policy. Richard Perle and David Wurmser have written position papers for Benjamin Netanyahu, who was hoping to return to his previous post as prime minister of Israel as the candidate of the right-wing Likud Party. So intimate a degree of involvement in the politics of a foreign country was once unusual in a civil servant, especially one employed by the Department of Defense and entrusted with the security and interests of the American nation. Traditionally those who have served the American people in the civil service, as in the military, regarded that service as precluding all others. That principle still holds, in most cases, but not in this one.

Anyone who questions the identification of America with Israel is routinely met with accusations of anti-Semitism. This extends to criticism of the Likud Party and policy, of the Sharon regime, of policy toward the Palestinians. America shares the West's history of anti-Semitism, and knows anti-Semitism in the present. When one fears that such a history might be reawakened, it is wise to exercise care in criticism. That care should not be made a license for the persecution of others.

From the time I first came to Chicago to the present day, I have seen Arabs and Muslims made the targets of unrestrained persecution, especially among the Straussians. At school, Straussian students told me that Arabs were dirty, they were animals, they were vermin. Now I read in Straussian books and articles, in editorials and postings on websites, that Arabs are violent, they are barbarous, they are the enemies of civilization, they are Nazis. Jaffa writes, "The Palestinian Authority, like the Nazis, is a gangster regime." Negotiating with the Palestinians is tantamount to negotiating with Hitler, Jaffa writes, an "imbecility." Islam is the religion of the sword. One need not be a scholar to remember that the root of "Islam" is the word for peace, *salaam*.

Among the most disturbing instances of this all too common bigotry is a book written by men who have served in two presidential administrations, David Frum and Richard Perle. *An End to Evil: How to Win the War Against Terror* has a strange familiarity about it. Scholars familiar with the language of anti-Semitism will find it reminiscent of older, long-dishonored texts. The careful fabrication, the language of blood libel, the calls for violence in the name of defense, all are present here. Frum and Perle tell us that though others are too timid to say so, the enemy is Islam. They tell us that Islam is a religion of terror, that Muslims make women slaves. Militant Muslims are terrorists "and though it is comforting to deny it" they are supported by moderate Muslims throughout the world, "including Muslim minorities in the West."

Muslims are dangerous, they tell us, and Americans must "police" their Muslim neighbors. No Muslim can be trusted: not the professor, not the FBI agent, not your neighbor. All must be watched. All are dangerous. The Muslim parents next door may be the ones who kill their daughter. Your colleague may be sending money to Islamic Jihad. You must stand with your neighbors against the dangers of Muslims, whose loyalty is always suspect. "American society must communicate a clear message to its Muslim citizens and residents, a clear message about what is expected of them." You must learn to distrust not only Muslims but their "fellow travelers in the non-Muslim West."

Perle and Frum and their Straussian colleagues have abandoned reason and study, democratic ideals and philosophic principle for a simpler, less honorable, but all too familiar world. Once it was another set of Semites who could not be trusted, whose primary loyalties lay elsewhere, who needed to be given a clear message about what was expected of them. Once, at the end of the nineteenth century, it was the Jewish anarchist and the Jewish communist who were portrayed as agents of global terror. Now it is Muslims who are involved in shadowy global conspiracies, Muslims who have "fellow travelers." The old language of anti-Semitism has found another target.

America and Israel must stand against Islam. "Mullahs and imams incited violence and slaughter against Christians and Jews," Frum and Perle declare. Terrorists are "rallying the Muslim world to jihad." Frum and Perle are doing the same. The United States must "end the terrorist regime in Syria," secure the "overthrow of the terrorist mullahs in Iran," and then cast an appraising eye on "Saudi Arabia and France not as friends but as rivals—maybe enemies." "There is no middle way for Americans: it is victory or holocaust." But whose will be the holocaust?

The American and European presses, and the American and European intelligentsia, have given prolonged and profound attention to the rise (or resurgence, or return) of anti-Semitism in Europe. The election (and reelection) of Jörg Haider in Austria has suggested that old prejudices have present electoral power. Acts of violence and vandalism in schools and synagogues show the persistence of popular bigotry. We are concerned, but neither we nor the Europeans feel all the concern we should. We ignore potent forms of anti-Semitism both at home and abroad. We fail to recognize the ways in which American policy exacerbates it.

We are troubled when graffiti against Jews appear on a European wall, but indifferent, like the Europeans themselves, to the burning of mosques. We are troubled when *Le Figaro* tells us that 9 percent of the French express "antipathy" toward Jews, but unconcerned that more than twice as many (19 percent) express antipathy toward Arab and Muslim North Africans. We are troubled when anger against Israel prompts anti-Semitic statements, but we are indifferent or apologetic when anger against Muslims expresses itself in anti-Semitic legislation. The just fear of an old peril for Jews has been used to license intolerance, incite violence, and make other people, Arab and Muslim, the objects of legal discrimination and popular hatred. In condemning the rise of anti-Semitism against Jews in Europe and remaining silent before the persecution of Arabs and Muslims, Americans not only license European discrimination, we indulge our own.

In America, anti-Semitism takes the Arab as its target more frequently than it takes the Jew. Anti-Semitism against Jews remains, but it is publicly and popularly condemned. Anti-Semitism against Arabs is tolerated, and occasionally encouraged. The former leader of the Southern Baptist Convention called the Prophet Muhammad a "demon-possessed pedophile." Franklin Graham, who prayed at George W. Bush's inauguration, referred to Islam as "an evil religion." Orthodox women who cover their hair are not criticized, or even much noticed. A Muslim woman who covers her hair may lose her job. Her choice is a matter of debate, and often public condemnation. Muslim men (or men whose turbans marked them as Muslim in the eyes of the ignorant) have been beaten and killed. We are horrified if we see a swastika, but indifferent to the manufacture of T-shirts and bumper stickers bearing anti-Semitic images of Arabs. We are troubled by anti-Semitism in Europe, but we have troubles of our own here.

First among these is our failure to confront our anti-Arab, anti-Muslim anti-Semitism. "Anti-Semitism," I have been told, is not a word that can be applied to discrimination against Arabs. The aversion to this broader, and more accurate, use has a double imperative: it constructs Arabs as alien, unlike ourselves, unlike our neighbors, and it conceals the historic antecedents of discrimination against them. Arabs are Semites and Arabic is a Semitic language. Anti-Semitism may take the form of religious or racial persecution, and often alternates between the two. As Jews were constructed as a different race, and condemned for deicide,

Arabs are now constructed as another race and Islam is made a "religion of terror." The caricatures that once served for one now serve the other. Still, many refuse to call these acts by their proper name.

Recognizing anti-Semitism against Arabs would oblige us to recognize that we tolerate, daily, the anti-Semitism we condemn in others. Condemnations of European anti-Semitism would have to take second place to an examination of our own. We would have to face the fact that our tolerance of anti-Semitism has placed people in danger, and the possibility that it might lead to other, greater dangers. Some of those dangers are already upon us.

America's intimate and unquestioning relation with Israel has enabled Americans to do both good and evil. We remember the Holocaust, we say that such a thing must never happen again, and in the protection of Israel we put our hands to that work. In doing so, however, we have put our hands to other work as well. We have licensed anti-Semitism at home and funded it abroad, on the condition that it take the Arab rather than the Jew as its target. We have put our hand to the persecution of Arabs and Muslims. In the nineteenth century, pogroms were assaults on another neighborhood, another village. In the twenty-first, pogroms are conducted abroad. Full recognition of the forms of American anti-Semitism would oblige us to consider the ways in which our own anti-Semitism has directed American foreign policy, blinding us to principles of democratic self-rule and national self-determination for the Palestinians, and impelling irrational and unjust wars. It would oblige us to consider the shameful way in which we have used opposition to one form of anti-Semitism as a license for another, and to recognize that we have made that bigotry the unacknowledged cornerstone of American foreign policy.

The idealization of the state of Israel was the work of Straussians, not of Strauss. The alliance with Christian fundamentalists in a latter-day crusade against Islam was the work of Straussians, not of Strauss. Strauss accepts and aligns himself with the distinction between "Israel" and "the Jewish state." He maintains that distinction in the last essay of his last book, composed in the last year of his life. In that essay Strauss returns to the work of Hermann Cohen, in a book entitled *Religion of Reason: Out of the Sources of Judaism*. When Strauss was young, Cohen was "the center of attraction for philosophically minded Jews who were devoted to Judaism." He was a figure of the late Enlightenment, an inspiration to many German Jews in a time when faith in the Enlightenment was fading. In this final essay, Strauss reaffirms Judaism as the religion of reason. In doing so, he departs from the understanding of Israel as a Jewish state.

In the essay Strauss turns away from the desire to be as the nations, to establish a homeland for the Jews. Instead he affirms that "Israel, the eternal people, is the symbol of mankind." Israel in this sense survives the "destruction of the Jewish state" and does not require its restoration. One can wish for such a state, work to establish and maintain it. One can see in Israel the fulfillment of hope and labor. For Strauss, the greatest achievement of the Jews lies elsewhere. Strauss writes, "The Jewish state as one state among many would not point as unmistakably to the unity of mankind as the one stateless people dedicated uniquely to the service of the unique God, the Lord of the whole earth." The "ideal Israel"—that is to say, the Israel of our hopes, the Israel of the idea—does exactly that. Monotheism contained within it an affirmation of the fundamental likeness and unity of human beings. "The patriotism of the prophets is at bottom nothing but universalism."

In the last year of his life, Leo Strauss asked that certain essays be collected, arranged in a particular order, and published under the title *Studies in Platonic Political Philosophy*. "Jerusalem and Athens" occupies a central place in that work. The book's title might seem to be a puzzle, for few of the essays deal directly with the works of Plato. Much earlier, in *On Tyranny*, Strauss had given an answer. He asked, "In what does philosophic politics consist?" and answered, "In satisfying the city that the philosophers are not atheists, that they do not desecrate everything sacred to the city, that they reverence what the city reverences, that they are not subversives, in short that they are not irresponsible adventurers, but the best of citizens." Plato's philosophic politics was, Strauss wrote, a "resounding success" that continued after him. "What Plato did in the Greek city and for it," Strauss wrote, "was done in and for Rome by Cicero. . . . It was done in and for the Islamic world by Farabi and in and for Judaism by Maimonides." These men, Plato, Cicero, al Farabi, and Maimonides, defended philosophy, made a place for it in the city, in the political. This is philosophic politics. Political philosophy may have a different end and form, but it bears a family resemblance to this enterprise.

All Straussians, all students of political theory, and well-read people throughout the world know that as he lay dying, Socrates' final concern was to settle his debts. "I owe a cock to Aesclepius." These final words have been much studied. Some argue that Socrates, in offering a gift to the god of healing, was suggesting that he saw death as a release. Socrates did not fear death, and may even have looked forward to it with some curiosity, but it is difficult, after reading the dialogues, to imagine him thinking of life as a disease. Socrates talked and drank, argued and feasted, fought for the Athenians and debated with them, took part, with often outrageous enthusiasm, in the life of the city. What we do know from the text is that Socrates felt that he had a debt and wished to settle it, and that the debt was to "the gods the city reverences." The essay that closes *Studies in Platonic Political Philosophy* may come in payment of a similar debt. In this essay, Strauss may be paying a debt: to a particular man, to Judaism, to revelation, perhaps to the God the city reverences. The last lines of the essay and the work are "It is a blessing for us that Hermann Cohen lived and wrote."

Strauss is grateful for Hermann Cohen's book, and his own book ends with thanks. Strauss has a debt to Judaism. "Truthfulness or intellectual probity animates Judaism in general and Jewish medieval philosophy, which always recognized the authority of reason, in particular." Strauss has a debt to the God the city reverences, the God sought by the unsatisfied desire for truth, the God whose worship acknowledges the limits of the reach of the human mind and heart. The book accomplishes the task of philosophical politics—to reconcile the city to philosophy—by showing that philosophers reverence the god the city reverences. Strauss pays these debts. He has, however, done something more. The book takes on the task of political philosophy, leading the city to question, giving its first allegiance not to revelation but to reason.

In the form of the book, in the placement of the essay, in the time of its composition, in the manner of its coming into the world, reason and revelation, politics and religion, are reconciled. An old text is newly opened, and one hears echoes of an enduring history, and something more. The book affirms the meaning of suffering, of Israel as the witness to the one God. The book affirms the oneness of God. The book affirms, as the prophets did, the oneness of mankind. In the end the essay is a form of the *Shema*, the prayer Jews recite as they face death: "Hear, O Israel, the Lord is our God, the Lord is One."

13 *The School of Baghdad*

We have faced death with Leo Strauss. Now we must face death in another place.

The Platonic political philosophy that Strauss made his life's work begins for him with al Farabi. Farabi, as Strauss called him, was the first of the Platonic political philosophers. Farabi teaches how to write in a time and place hostile to philosophy. In that hostile place, Farabi taught politics and philosophy to his students, and to Strauss.

Strauss took Farabi as his teacher, but he was also kindred and compatriot. Farabi writes that though it is unlikely that all the attributes of the philosopher and ruler will be found in one man, it may be that within a single city, the qualities necessary for politics and philosophy may exist scattered among the people. This makes an admirable democracy possible. Farabi also writes that though it is unlikely that there will be a city of philosophers (that would be the most admirable of democratic cities), philosophers scattered in time and space nevertheless form a city of their own. Strauss calls it, after al Farabi, "the city of speech." Thus Strauss and al Farabi find themselves in the same city. Their teachings echo in another city. Al Farabi taught in Baghdad.

Strauss's philosophy thus begins where our politics ends, at least for the moment. Our story ends here, as the city where Farabi taught Strauss is occupied by those who call themselves his students.

I have told you the story in which Strauss says, "I am a Jew as Maimonides is a Jew." There is another story about Strauss and Maimonides (perhaps many more). In this one, a student asks Strauss in what time and place he would like to have lived. Strauss responds that he would like to have lived in the time and place of Maimonides, except that he would have missed Nietzsche.

In this respect, as in so many others, Strauss's teaching ran against the sensibilities of his most ardent disciples. Strauss places himself in an Arab court, under the rule of the man who defeated Christendom, and gives as his only regret missing the favorite German (however undeservedly) of the anti-Semites. What can this mean?

Maimonides was a physician and philosopher at the court of Yusuf ibn Ayyub, Salah ad-Din, called Saladin in the West, the conqueror of Jerusalem. In the West, Saladin is remembered as an honorable man. Disraeli, perhaps a Jew, perhaps a Christian, but certainly a statesman and a conservative, wrote Saladin into his romance *Tancred*. We have the memoirs of Saladin's secretary, whose attention to detail redeems his occasional inability to recognize the full greatness of the man he loved. Children who dream of Richard the Lionheart face disillusionment with age and learning. Saladin remains. When the Christians took the city of Jerusalem, al Quds, the streets ran with blood and there was no ransoming of prisoners. Saladin took the city with restraint. Prisoners were ransomed, and when the Crusaders could come up with no more money, Saladin paid the ransoms himself. There were Christians and Jews in Saladin's forces and on his staff. Maimonides was Saladin's physician. These things have been remembered and honored in the Islamic world as well. An old Egyptian film, made under Nasser, has Richard listening to Christmas carols sung in the Jerusalem of Saladin.

Cairo in Saladin's time is akin to Andalusia at its height. In it Muslims, Christians, and Jews lived, worked, and studied together. The generous and the intellectual among Muslims, Christians, and Jews still remember Andalusia with affection and regret. Youssef Chahine's film *Destiny* recalls the struggle for philosophy through Ibn Sina, the philosopher known to Europe as Avicenna, whose work taught Thomas Aquinas and other Christians central to European philosophy. Tariq Ali's novel *Shadow of the Pomegranate Tree* looks sadly on the time when the once-romanced *reconquista* drove Muslim and Jew from Spain and imprisoned Christians in a much-diminished world. Many have written of the glory of Andalusia and of all that was lost to faith and reason with the reconquista. People of goodwill, Christians, Muslims, and Jews, look back to Andalusia as if to a common homeland.

This moment, and Strauss's regard for it, stand as a reproach to those who would set the West against Islam. Neither Islam nor Judaism is alien to Strauss's conception of the West. Neither Judaism nor Islam is alien to America. Both belong to the idea of the West as the evening land, the place where the world is to be made again, healed and made whole.

Before Strauss and Cropsey's *History of Political Philosophy*, the dominant account of the history of political philosophy came from George Sabine. Sabine's is an entirely European work, and in the narrowest sense. There are no accounts of Muslim or Jewish philosophers. Political philosophy is presented as an entirely Christian enterprise—and a Christianity alienated from the other children of Abraham. The reliance of Christians on al Farabi for the transmission and the understanding of Plato and Aristotle is forgotten. The debt of Aquinas to ibn Rushd, Averroës, is too great to be overlooked. He appears, however, not as a philosopher but as a school. The school is presented not as the work of Arab Muslims but in its derivative (or corrected) form as "Latin Averroëism." In Strauss and Cropsey, things are otherwise. There are chapters on Plato, Aristotle, and Kant, and there are chapters on al Farabi and Maimonides. The chapter on Marsilius of Padua, written by Strauss himself, notes the importance of ibn Rushd to an understanding of Christian and European thought.

Strauss revived the study of Islamic philosophy among political theorists in the West. In *Persecution and the Art of Writing,* as Strauss makes the argument that would make him famous, he observes that the sociology of knowledge in the West has been crippled in its understanding of philosophy. It has failed, Strauss writes, because of "the inadequacy of its historical information." All Westerners knew, he writes reproachfully, was the West. "The present writer," he says of himself, came to his own understanding "while he was studying the Jewish and Islamic philosophy of the Middle Ages."

Strauss's work, from his earliest writings to the last, is filled with references to Muslim theorists. His students took that learning further. Strauss wrote on al Farabi. Ralph Lerner and Muhsin Mahdi published a reader on medieval political thought in which Jewish, Christian, and Muslim philosophers were joined. One could read al Ghazali and al Farabi, ibn Rushd and ibn Tufayl. There is still no collection to surpass it in English. Lerner himself wrote on ibn Rushd and Maimonides. Charles Butterworth wrote on al Farabi and later on ibn Khaldun, al Afghani, and the constitutional tradition in Islam. The contributing scholars were Jewish, Christian, and Muslim. In their preface, Lerner and Mahdi wrote, "We have tried to look at this vast medieval literature with eyes uninformed by any prejudgment, however scholarly, that would assure us in advance that political philosophy could not conceivably be found in the writings of this particular man or of this particular religious community."

The conception of philosophy, the breadth of learning found in Strauss and among his students stands in sharp contrast to the stubborn ignorance of the Straussians. Strauss reproaches Western intellectuals for their limited vision, their inattention to thought outside their understanding of the West. The Straussians take pride in their narrowness. Strauss and certain of his students opened the West to an understanding of itself in and through the East, through Judaic and Islamic philosophy. The Straussians have set themselves to guard the gates Strauss opened: they struggle to keep the West confined, to keep scholars and scholarship within bounds, to keep out philosophers they never wish to read. They have not kept faith with learning.

The meeting of Islam and the West can be cast as Kristol and Kagan cast it, as "defenders of civilization against civilization's opponents." It can be cast as George W. Bush cast it, as a crusade. Nothing in Strauss's writing endorses a Judeo-Christian crusade against Islam. Strauss saw Jewish and Muslim philosophy as closely linked, especially as they were made clear by Maimonides and al Farabi. The gift of Judaism is the text. If one considers Strauss's reading of al Farabi, one can see Judaism and Islam, reason and revelation, meeting on common ground. The idea of the city looking for wisdom, the city seeking to establish justice, animates the writings of the Greeks. In this place, not only Strauss and Arendt but al Farabi and Locke, Maimonides and Rousseau, find common ground. Islam and the West find common ground in the imagined city of the Greeks.

Al Farabi wrote of America before America was born. The democratic city, he writes, is not a perfect city, but of all the ignorant cities of this world it is the "most admirable and happy city." "On the surface, it looks like an embroidered garment full of colored figures and dyes. Everybody loves it and loves to reside in it, because there is no human wish or desire that this city does not satisfy. The nations emigrate to it and reside there, and it grows beyond measure. People of every race multiply in it, and this by all kinds of copulation and marriages, resulting in children of extremely varied dispositions, with extremely varied education and up-bringing. Consequently, this city develops into many cities, distinct yet intertwined, with the parts of each scattered through the parts of the others. Strangers cannot be distinguished from the residents. All kinds of wishes and ways of life are to be found in it." This city is not without dangers. Because it is ignorant, the city can only hope to follow the example of Socrates, to know that it does not know. This city, because of all that it contains within it, "possesses both good and evil to a greater degree than the rest of the ignorant cities." Yet it is only in this city, and because of these dangers, that both democracy and philosophy are possible. Al Farabi writes, "The bigger, the more civilized, the more populated, the more productive, and the more perfect it is the more prevalent and the greater are the good and evil it possesses." So it is for us.

In democracy nothing is certain. We democrats go willingly into the evening land, not knowing who will rule after the next election, never certain of what the future will bring us. So it is with philosophy. Faith brings certainty, reason a question. Philosophy is a "pure and whole questioning." Democracy and philosophy find common ground in the quest and the question. What is justice? What does it mean to be an American?

These are the questions on the ground in Baghdad.

Index

Index